Carl Friedrich Gauss
Galois
Thales
Archimedes
Bhaskara I
Aryabhatta
Grigori Perelman
René Descartes
Euclid
Georg Cantor
Pierre-Simon Laplace
Ada Lovelace
David Hilbert
Isaac Newton
Henri Poincaré
Leonhard Euler
Bernhard Riemann
Blaise Pascal
Pythagoras
Bhaskara II
Brahmagupta
Emmy Noether
Eratosthenes
George Boole
David Hilbert
Srinivasa Ramanujan
Andrew Wiles
John von Neumann
Alan Turing
Pierre de Fermat

PROBLEMS IN SCHOOL MATHEMATICS

Problem-Solving in School Mathematics: Unraveling the
Challenges and Building Foundations

HIMADRI CHAKRABORTY

NewDelhi • London

BLUEROSE PUBLISHERS
India | U.K.

Copyright © Himadri Chakraborty 2025

All rights reserved by author. No part of this publication may be reproduced, stored in a retrieval system or transmitted in any form or by any means, electronic, mechanical, photocopying, recording or otherwise, without the prior permission of the author. Although every precaution has been taken to verify the accuracy of the information contained herein, the publisher assumes no responsibility for any errors or omissions. No liability is assumed for damages that may result from the use of information contained within.

BlueRose Publishers takes no responsibility for any damages, losses, or liabilities that may arise from the use or misuse of the information, products, or services provided in this publication.

For permissions requests or inquiries regarding this publication, please contact:

BLUEROSE PUBLISHERS
www.BlueRoseONE.com
info@bluerosepublishers.com
+91 8882 898 898
+4407342408967

ISBN: 978-93-6783-000-0

Cover design: Manisha Debnath
Typesetting: Himadri Chakraborty

First Edition: Februray 2025

पिताधर्मः पिता स्वर्गः पिता हि परमं तपः।
पितरि प्रीतिमापन्ने प्रीयन्ते सर्वदेवताः॥
पितरौ यस्य तृप्यन्ति सेवया च गुणेन च।
तस्य भागीरथी स्नानमहन्यहनि वर्त्तते॥
सर्वतीर्थमयी माता सर्वदेवमयः पिता।
मातरं पितरं तस्मात्सर्वयत्नेन पूजयेत्॥
मातरं पितरं चैव यस्तु कुर्यात्प्रदक्षिणम्।
प्रदक्षिणीकृता तेन सप्तदीपा वसुन्धरा॥

For my parents
(Swapan Chakraborty & Rekha Saha Chakraborty),
whose love and wisdom continue to guide me.

FOUNDATION

Topic	Interpretation
Natural Number	Positive counting numbers starting from 1
Whole Number	Non-negative numbers starting from 0
Integers	Positive, negative and zero
Rational Numbers	Numbers that can be expressed as a fraction of two integers
Irrational Numbers	Numbers that cannot be expressed as a fraction
Real Numbers	All numbers on the number line (both rational and irrational)
Average	$\dfrac{Sum\ of\ all\ values}{Number\ of\ values}$
Ratio	$\dfrac{Quantity\ A}{Quantity\ B}$
Percentage	$\left(\dfrac{Part}{Whole}\right) \times 100$
Profit & Loss	$Profit\ Percentage = \dfrac{Selling\ Price - Cost\ Price}{Cost\ Price} \times 100$ $Loss\ Percentage = \dfrac{Cost\ Price - Selling\ Price}{Cost\ Price} \times 100$
Simple Interest (SI)	$\dfrac{Principle \times Rate\ of\ Interset\ Per\ Year \times Time\ in\ Years}{100}$
Compound Interest	$Amount = Principle\left(1 + \dfrac{Rate\ of\ interest}{100}\right)^{Time\ in\ Years}$
Speed, Time and Distance	$Speed = \dfrac{Distance}{Time}$
Water Current	Downstream Speed = Speed of the Boat in Still Water + Speed of the Stream Upstream Speed = Speed of the Boat in Still Water − Speed of the Stream
Work	Rate of Work × Time
Partnership	$\dfrac{Partner's\ Investment \times Time\ Period}{\sum(All\ Partner's\ Investment \times Time\ Period)} \times Total\ Profit$
Mixture	Concentration of Mixture $= \dfrac{\sum(Amount\ of\ Each\ Substance\ \times\ Concentration\ of\ Each)}{Total\ Amount\ of\ Mixture}$

Bracket Type	Symbol	Primary Uses	Secondary Uses
Parentheses	( )	Order of operations, function arguments	Grouping or explicit multiplication
Square Brackets	[ ]	Grouping inside parentheses, intervals	Matrices, vectors or sequences
Curly Braces	{ }	Sets, piecewise functions	Proofs or collections of objects
Angle Brackets	⟨ ⟩	Inner product in vector spaces	Represent tuples, quantum mechanics
Vertical Bars	| |	Denote absolute values, represent determinants of matrices	Show cardinality of sets, indicate norms or magnitudes
Double Brackets	⟦ ⟧	Logic, semantics	Rarely used outside specialized

Contents

THREE DIMENSIONAL SHAPES 1

ALGEBRA 5

GEOMETRY 58

MENSURATION 87

SEQUENCE & SERIES 100

COORDINATE GEOMETRY 107

TRIGONOMETRY 127

CALCULUS 150

VECTOR ALGEBRA 176

PROBABILITY 186

PROBLEMS IN SCHOOL MATHEMATICS

THREE DIMENSIONAL SHAPES

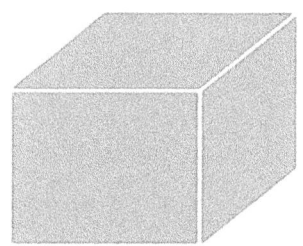

Cube (6 Faces, 12 Edges, 8 Vertices)

Cuboid (6 Faces, 12 Edges, 8 Vertices)

Cylinder (2 Faces & 1 Curved Surface, 2 Edges, 0 Vertices)

PROBLEMS IN SCHOOL MATHEMATICS

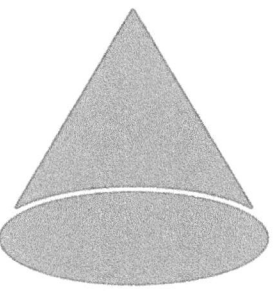

Cone (1 Face & 1 Curved Surface, 1 Edge, 1 Vertex)

Sphere (1 Curved Surface, 0 Edges, 0 Vertices)

Torus (1 curved Surface, 0 Edges, 0 Vertices)

PROBLEMS IN SCHOOL MATHEMATICS

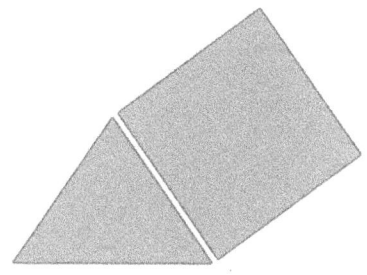

Triangular Prism (5 Faces, 9 Edges, 6 Vertices)

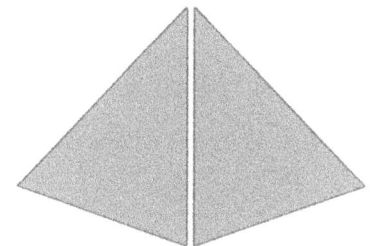

Square Based Pyramid (5 Faces, 8 Edges, 5 Vertices)

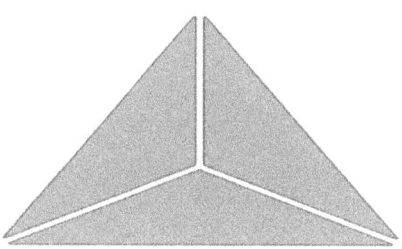

Tetrahedron (4 Faces, 6 Edges, 4 Vertices)

PROBLEMS IN SCHOOL MATHEMATICS

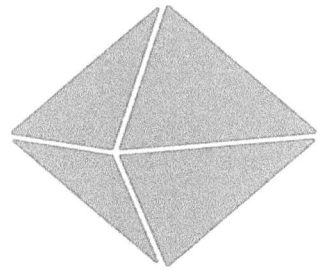

Octahedron (8 Faces, 12 Edges, 6 Vertices)

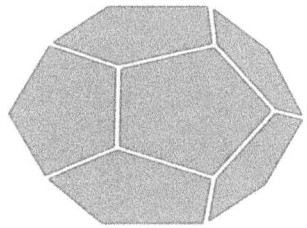

Dodecahedron (12 Faces, 30 Edges, 20 Vertices)

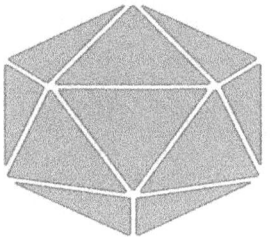

Icosahedron (20 Faces, 30 Edges, 12 Vertices)

ALGEBRA

2. Algebra
Algebra is a branch of mathematics dealing with symbols and the rules for manipulating those symbols.

2.1. (Algebra) Polynomial
A polynomial is a mathematical expression involving a sum of powers of variables multiplied by coefficients. The general form of a polynomial in one variable x is:
$a_n x^n + a_{n-1} x^{n-1} + \ldots a_1 x + a_0$, where
$a_n, a_{n-1}, \ldots a_1, a_0$ are constants called coefficients, and n is non-negative integer representing the degree of the polynomial.

Term	Definition	General Form
Monomial	A polynomial with only one term	ax^n
Binomial	A polynomial with exactly two terms	$ax^n + bx^m$
Trinomial	A polynomial with exactly three terms	$ax^n + bx^m + cx^k$
Constant Polynomial	A polynomial with degree 0 (no variable, just a constant)	a_0
Linear Polynomial	A polynomial of degree 1	$ax + b$
Quadratic Polynomial	A polynomial of degree 2	$ax^2 + bx + c$
Cubic Polynomial	A polynomial of degree 3	$ax^3 + bx^2 + cx + d$
Quartic Polynomial	A polynomial of degree 4	$ax^4 + bx^3 + \cdots + e$
Quintic Polynomial	A polynomial of degree 5	$ax^5 + bx^4 + \cdots + f$

PROBLEMS IN SCHOOL MATHEMATICS

2.1.1. (Algebra) (Polynomial) Addition
$x - a = b$
Or, $x - a + a = b + a$
Or, $x = b + a$

2.1.2. (Algebra) (Polynomial) Subtraction
$x + a = b$
Or, $x + a - a = b - a$
Or, $x = b - a$

2.1.3 (Algebra) (Polynomial) Multiplication
$\frac{x}{a} = b$
Or, $a\frac{x}{a} = ab$
Or, $x = ab$

2.1.4. (Algebra) (Polynomial) Division
$ax = b$
Or, $\frac{a}{a}x = \frac{b}{a}$
Or, $x = \frac{b}{a}$

2.1.5. (Algebra) (Polynomial) Inversion
$\frac{1}{x} = a$
Or, $x = \frac{1}{a}$

2.1.6. (Algebra) (Polynomial) Squaring
$\sqrt{x} = a$
Or, $x = a^2$

PROBLEMS IN SCHOOL MATHEMATICS

2.1.7. (Algebra) (Polynomial) Square Root
$x^2 = a$
Or, $x = \pm\sqrt{a}$

2.1.8. (Algebra) (Polynomial) Natural Log
$e^x = a$
Or, $\ln(e^x) = \ln a$
Or, $x = \ln a$

2.1.9. (Algebra) (Polynomial) Exponentials
$\ln x = a$
Or, $e^{\ln x} = e^a$
Or, $x = e^a$

2.1.10. (Algebra) (Polynomial) Order of Operations
$Bracket\,(\,)\,or\,\{\,\}\,or\,[\,]$
$Order\,or\,Power\,x^n\,or\,\sqrt{x}$
$Division \div$
$Multiplication \times$
$Addition +$
$Subtraction -$

2.1.11. (Algebra) (Polynomial) Commutative Property of Addition and Multiplication
$a + b = b + a\,and\,ab = ba$

2.1.12. (Algebra) (Polynomial) Associative Property of Addition and Multiplication
$a + (b + c) = (a + b) + c\,and\,a(bc) = (ab)c$

2.1.13. (Algebra) (Polynomial) Distributive Property of Multiplication over Addition
$a(b + c) = ab + ac\,and\,(b + c)a = ba + ca$

PROBLEMS IN SCHOOL MATHEMATICS

2.1.14. (Algebra) (Polynomial) Identities in Addition and Multiplication
$0 + a = a + 0 = a$ and $1 \times a = a \times 1 = a$

2.1.15. (Algebra) (Polynomial) Inverse in Addition and Multiplication
$a + (-a) = (-a) + a = 0$ and $a \times \frac{1}{a} = \frac{1}{a} \times a = 1$

2.1.16. (Algebra) (Polynomial) Product of two Binomials
$(x + a)(x + b) = x^2 + (a + b)x + ab$

2.1.17. (Algebra) (Polynomial) Square of a Binomial
$(a + b)^2 = a^2 + 2ab + b^2 = (a - b)^2 + 4ab$
$(a - b)^2 = a^2 - 2ab + b^2 = (a + b)^2 - 4ab$

2.1.18. (Algebra) (Polynomial) Sum of Squares
$a^2 + b^2 = (a + b)^2 - 2ab = (a - b)^2 + 2ab$

2.1.19. (Algebra) (Polynomial) Difference of Squares
$a^2 - b^2 = (a + b)(a - b)$

2.1.20. (Algebra) (Polynomial) Cube of a Binomial
$$(a - b)^3 = a^3 - b^3 - 3ab(a - b)$$
$$= a^3 - 3a^2b + 3ab^2 - b^3$$
$$(a + b)^3 = a^3 + b^3 + 3ab(a + b)$$
$$= a^3 + 3a^2b + 3ab^2 + b^3$$

2.1.21. (Algebra) (Polynomial) Sum of Cubes
$$a^3 + b^3 = (a + b)(a^2 - ab + b^2)$$
$$= (a + b)^3 - 3ab(a + b)$$

2.1.22. (Algebra) (Polynomial) Difference of Cubes
$$a^3 - b^3 = (a - b)(a^2 + ab + b^2)$$
$$= (a - b)^3 + 3ab(a - b)$$

2.1.23. (Algebra) (Polynomial) Square of a Trinomial
$$(a + b + c)^2 = a^2 + b^2 + c^2 + 2ab + 2bc + 2ca$$

2.1.24. (Algebra) (Polynomial) Cube of a Trinomial
$$(a + b + c)^3 = a^3 + b^3 + c^3 + 3(a + b)(b + c)(c + a)$$

2.1.25. (Algebra) (Polynomial) Sum of Cubes of Three quantities minus three Times their Product
$$a^3 + b^3 + c^3 - 3abc$$
$$= (a + b + c)(a^2 + b^2 + c^2 - ab - bc - ca)$$

2.1.26. (Algebra) (Polynomial) Zeros of the Quadratic Polynomial
α and β are the zeros of polynomial $p(x) = ax^2 + bx + c$
$$\alpha + \beta = -\frac{b}{a} \text{ and } \alpha\beta = \frac{c}{a}$$

2.1.27. (Algebra) (Polynomial) Zeros of the Cubic Polynomial
α, β and γ are the zeros of polynomial
$p(x) = ax^3 + bx^2 + cx + d$
$$\alpha + \beta + \gamma = -\frac{b}{a}$$
$$\alpha\beta + \beta\gamma + \gamma\alpha = \frac{c}{a}$$
$$\alpha\beta\gamma = -\frac{d}{a}$$

PROBLEMS IN SCHOOL MATHEMATICS

2.1.28. (Algebra) (Polynomial) Nature of Roots
Polynomial $p(x) = ax^2 + bx + c$
Two real roots, if $b^2 - 4ac \geq 0$
Real roots are $\frac{-b \pm \sqrt{b^2 - 4ac}}{2a}$
Two distinct real roots, if $b^2 - 4ac > 0$
Two equal real roots, if $b^2 - 4ac = 0$
No real roots, if $b^2 - 4ac < 0$

2.1.29. (Algebra) (Polynomial) Remainder Theorem
When a polynomial $f(x)$ is divided by $(x - a)$, the remainder is $f(a)$.

2.1.30 (Algebra) (Polynomial) Factor Theorem
If $f(x)$ is a polynomial and $f(a) = 0$, then $(x - a)$ is a factor of $f(x)$.
If $(x - a)$ is a factor of $f(x)$, then $f(a) = 0$.

2.1.31 (Algebra) (Polynomial) Law of Indices
- **_Product Rule:_** $a^m \times a^n = a^{m+n}$
- **_Quotient Rule:_** $\frac{a^m}{a^n} = a^{m-n}$
- **_Power of a Power Rule:_** $(a^m)^n = a^{mn}$
- **_Power of a Product Rule:_** $(ab)^m = a^m \times b^m$
- **_Power of a Quotient Rule:_** $\left(\frac{a}{b}\right)^m = \frac{a^m}{b^m}$
- **_Zero Exponent Rule:_** $a^0 = 1$ (for $a \neq 0$)
- **_Negative Exponent Rule:_** $a^{-m} = \frac{1}{a^m}$ (for $a \neq 0$)
- **_Root Exponent Rule:_**
$$\sqrt[\frac{m}{n}]{\frac{ab}{cd}} = \left(\frac{ab}{cd}\right)^{\frac{n}{m}} = \frac{(ab)^{\frac{n}{m}}}{(cd)^{\frac{n}{m}}} = \frac{(a)^{\frac{n}{m}} \cdot (b)^{\frac{n}{m}}}{(c)^{\frac{n}{m}} \cdot (d)^{\frac{n}{m}}}$$

2.2. (Algebra) Sets

In mathematics, a set is a collection of distinct objects, considered as an object in its own right. These objects can anything: numbers, letters, symbols, or even other sets. Sets are usually denoted with curly braces.

Elements of Set:
If a is an element of a set A, we written $a \in A$
If b is not an element of a set A, we written $b \notin A$

Representation of Set:
- **Roster/Tabular Form:** Elements of the set are listed explicitly.
- **Set-builder Form:** A set is described by a property that its members satisfy.

Cardinality: The number of elements in a set denoted $|A|$ for a set A.

2.2.1. (Algebra) (Sets) Types of Sets

The Empty Set: The empty set, also known as the null set or the void set is a set that contains no element. It is denoted by $\emptyset$ or $\{\}$.

Finite and Infinite Sets: A set is finite if it contains a countable number of elements.
A set is infinite if it contains an uncountable number of elements.

Equal Sets: Two sets are considered equal if they contain exactly the same elements. This means the every element of the first set must be an element of the second set, and every element of the second set must be an element of the first set.

Subsets: A subset is a set where every element is also an element of another set.

Proper Subset: *A set A is a proper subset of another set B if every element of A is also an element of B, and A is not equal to B. This is denoted as A⊂B.*

Superset: *A set B is a superset of another set A if B contains all the elements of A. This is denoted as B⊇A.*

Power Set: *The set of all subsets of a set A, including the empty set and A itself. If A has n elements, its power set contains 2^n subsets.*

Singleton Set: *A singleton set is a set that contains exactly one element.*

Universal Set: *A universal set is the set that contains all objects or elements under consideration for a particular discussion or problem. It is obtain denoted by U and includes all the elements that are relevant to a given context or set of sets.*

2.2.2. (Algebra) (Sets) Venn Diagrams

A Venn diagram is a visual tool used to show the relationships between different sets. It typically uses overlapping circles or other shapes to represent sets, with the overlaps illustrating common elements between the sets.

2.2.3. (Algebra) (Sets) Operation on Sets

Operation on sets involves various methods for combining, comparing and manipulating sets.

Common Operations Include:

Union $(A \cup B)$: *Combines all elements from both sets, removing duplicates.*

Intersection $(A \cap B)$: *Includes only elements that are in both sets. Sets A and B are disjoint if $A \cap B = \emptyset$.*

Difference $(A - B)$: *Contains elements in A but not in B.*

Symmetric Difference $(A \Delta B)$: *The set of elements in either A or B, but not in both.*
Complement $(A' = U - A)$: *Includes elements not in a given set, relative to the universal set.*
Cartesian Product $(A \times B)$: *The set of all ordered pairs (a, b), where $a \in A$ and $b \in B$.*

2.2.4. (Algebra) (Sets) Fundamental Laws

- **_Commutative Laws:_** $A \cup B = B \cup A$ and $A \cap B = B \cap A$
- **_Associative Laws:_** $(A \cup B) \cup C = A \cup (B \cup C)$ and $(A \cap B) \cap C = A \cap (B \cap C)$
- **_Distributive Laws:_** $A \cup (B \cap C) = (A \cup B) \cap (A \cup C)$ and $A \cap (B \cup C) = (A \cap B) \cup (A \cap C)$
- **_Identity Laws:_** $A \cup \emptyset = A$ and $A \cap U = A$
- **_Complement Laws:_** $A \cup A' = U$ and $A \cap A' = \emptyset$
- **_Idempotent Laws:_** $A \cup A = A$ and $A \cap A = A$
- **_Domination Laws:_** $A \cup U = U$ and $A \cap \emptyset = \emptyset$
- **_Double Complement Law:_** $(A')' = A$
- **_Absorption Laws:_** $A \cup (A \cap B) = A$ and $A \cap (A \cup B) = A$
- **_De Morgan's Law:_** $(A \cup B)' = A' \cup B'$ and $(A \cap B)' = A' \cup B'$
- **_Difference Laws:_** $A - A = \emptyset$, $U - A = A'$ and $A - B = A \cap B'$
- **_Symmetric Difference Laws:_** $A \Delta B = (A - B) \cup (B - A)$ and $A \Delta A = \emptyset$ and $A \Delta \emptyset = A$
- **_Cardinality of Union:_** $|A \cup B| = |A| + |B| - |A \cap B|$ and $|A \cup B \cup C| = |A| + |B| + |C| - |A \cap B| - |B \cap C| - |C \cap A| + |A \cap B \cap C|$
- **_Cardinality of Intersection:_** $|A \cap B| \leq min(|A|, |B|)$
- **_Cardinality of Difference:_** $|A - B| = |A| - |A \cap B|$
- **_Cardinality of Complement:_** $|A'| = |U| - |A|$
- **_Cardinality of Symmetric:_** $|A \Delta B| = |A| + |B| - 2|A \cap B|$

PROBLEMS IN SCHOOL MATHEMATICS

2.3. (Algebra) Relations & Functions
A relation and a function are concepts used to describe relationships between sets.

2.3.1. (Algebra) (Relations & Functions) Relation
A relation between two sets A and B is a set of ordered pairs where first element of each pair is from A and the second element from B.

2.3.2. (Algebra) (Relations & Functions) Function
A function is a specific type of relation where each element in the domain (set A) is related to exactly one element in the co-domain (set B). In other words, a function maps each input to exactly one output.

Term	Definition	Example for $f(x) = x^2$, $f: \mathbb{R} \to \mathbb{R}$
Domain	Set of all valid inputs	$\mathbb{R}$
Co-domain	Set of all potential outputs	$\mathbb{R}$
Range	Set of all actual outputs produced	$[0, \infty)$
Image	Output corresponding to specific input	Image of -2: 4
Pre-image	Set of inputs that produce a specific output	Pre-image of 4: $\{-2, 2\}$

PROBLEMS IN SCHOOL MATHEMATICS

2.3.3. (Algebra) (Relations & Functions) Mapping

Relation	Function
Many-to-many, one-to-one, or one-to-many possible	One-to-one or many-to-one only

2.3.4. (Algebra) (Relations & Functions) To Find the Domain and Range

Domain: The set of all possible input values (x) for which the function is defined.

- Identify Restriction:
  - If the function has a denominator, set it $\neq 0$ (to avoid division by zero).
  - If the function involves square roots (or even roots), ensure the radicand (expression inside the root) is ≥ 0 (to avoid imaginary numbers)
  - Check any logarithms, the argument of a log must be > 0.
- Solve these restrictions to determine valid values of 'x'.

Range: The set of all possible output values $(f(x))$ from the function.

- Analyze the function's behavior:
  - Look at how $f(x)$ behaves as x approaches boundaries of the domain (e.g., $+\infty, -\infty$, or domain limits).
  - Check for horizontal asymptotes or restrictions on output values.
- Graph or algebraically solve:
  - Graph the function to observe the y values it reaches.

- Solve for x in terms of y (inverse function method) to find y restrictions.

2.3.5. (Algebra) (Relations & Functions) Types of Relations

Empty Relation: *A relation where no elements from the domain are related to any elements in the co-domain.*

Universal Relation: *A relation where every element of the domain is related to every element of the co-domain.*

Identity Relation: *A relation where every element is related only to itself.*

Reflexive Relation: *A relation $\mathcal{R}$ on a set A is reflexive if every element is related to itself, i.e., $(a, a) \in \mathcal{R}$ for all $a \in A$*

Symmetric Relation: *A relation $\mathcal{R}$ on a set A is symmetric if $(a, b) \in \mathcal{R}$ implies $(b, a) \in \mathcal{R}$ for all $a, b \in A$.*

Anti-Symmetric Relation: *A relation $\mathcal{R}$ is anti-symmetric if $(a, b) \in \mathcal{R}$ and $(b, a) \in \mathcal{R}$ imply that $a = b$.*

Transitive Relation: *A relation $\mathcal{R}$ is transitive if $(a, b) \in \mathcal{R}$ and $(b, c) \in \mathcal{R}$ imply $(a, c) \in \mathcal{R}$.*

Equivalence Relation: *A relation that is reflexive, symmetric, and transitive.*

Partial Order Relation: *A relation that is reflexive, anti-symmetric, and transitive. This often used to model ordering (but not necessarily total orderings).*

Total Order (Linear Order) Relation: *A relation that is partial order and also satisfies the property that for any two elements a and b, either $a\mathcal{R}b$ or $b\mathcal{R}a$ (i.e., all elements are comparable).*

Inverse Relation: *The inverse of a relation $\mathcal{R}$ is a relation where the pairs (b, a) are related if $(a, b) \in \mathcal{R}$.*

Function (Special Type of Relation): *A relation where element of the domain is related to exactly one element of*

the co-domain. Every function is a relation, but not every relation is a function.
Trichotomy Relation: *A relation where for any two elements a and b , exactly one of these holds: $a\mathcal{R}b$, $b\mathcal{R}a$ or $a = b$*

2.3.6. (Algebra) (Relations & Functions) Types of Functions
One-to-One (Injective) Function: *A function where each element of the domain maps to a unique element of the range.*
Onto (Surjective) Function: *A function where every element in the range has at least one corresponding element in the domain.*
One-to-One Correspondence (Bijective) Function: *A function that has both injective and surjective, meaning each domain elements maps to a unique range element, and every range element has a corresponding domain element.*
Constant Function: *A function where every input maps to the same output.*
Identity Function: *A function where every element maps to itself.*
Linear Function: *A function of the form of $f(x) = ax + b$, where a and b are constants.*
Quadratic Function: *A function of the form of $f(x) = ax^2 + bx + c$, where a, b and c are constants.*
Polynomial Function: *A function that involves powers of x.*
Rational Function: *A function that is the ratio of two polynomials.*
Exponential Function: *A function of the form of $f(x) = a^x$, where a is a positive constant.*

Logarithmic Function: *The inverse of an exponential function.*
Trigonometric Function: *Functions based on angles, such as sine, cosine and tangent.*
Piecewise Function: *A function defined by different expressions in different intervals of the domain.*
Recursive Function: *A function that is defined in terms of itself.*
Implicit Function: *A function where the relationship between variables is not explicitly solved for one variable in terms of another.*

2.3.7. (Algebra) (Relations & Functions) Function Composition

Function composition involves combining two functions to form a new function. If you have two function f and g is written as $(f \circ g)(x)$, and it means applying $g(x)$ first, then applying f to the result of $g(x)$.
Definition: *If $f: B \to C$ and $g: A \to B$, then the composition $(f \circ g): A \to C$ is defined by:*
$(f \circ g)(x) = f(g(x))$
This means the output $g(x)$ is used as the input for $f(x)$.

2.3.8. (Algebra) (Relations & Functions) Invertible Function

An invertible function (or bijective function) is one that has an inverse, meaning you can 'undo' the function. A function f is invertible if and only if it is both injective (one-to-one) and surjective (onto).
Definition: *A function $f: A \to B$ has an inverse $f^{-1}: B \to A$ if: $f(f^{-1}(y)) = y$ for all $y \in B$ and*
$f(f^{-1}(x)) = x$ *for all $x \in A$*

2.4. (Algebra) Complex Numbers

Complex numbers are numbers that extend the real number system to include the square root of negative one, denoted as i. A complex number is expressed in the form of $a + ib$, where a and b are real numbers, and i is the imaginary with the property $i^2 = -1$.

2.4.1. (Algebra) (Complex Numbers) The Modulus and the Conjugate of Complex Number

For a complex number $z = a + bi$

Modulus: The modulus (or absolute value) of z is given by $|z| = \sqrt{a^2 + b^2}$. It represents the distance of the complex number from the origin in the complex plane.

Properties of Modulus:
- $|z| \geq 0$
- $|z_1 \times z_2| = |z_1| \times |z_2|$
- $\left|\frac{z_1}{z_2}\right| = \frac{|z_1|}{|z_2|}$ (assuming $z_2 \neq 0$)
- $|z_1 + z_2| \leq ||z_1| + |z_2||$
- $|z_1 - z_2| \geq ||z_1| - |z_2||$
- $|z^n| = |z|^n$

Conjugate: The conjugate of z is $\bar{z} = a - bi$. It is obtained by changing the sign of the imaginary part, and it reflects the complex number across the real axis.

Properties of Conjugate:
- $z \times \bar{z} = |z|^2$
- $\frac{z_1}{z_2} = \frac{z_1 \times \overline{z_2}}{z_2 \times \overline{z_2}} = \frac{z_1 \times \overline{z_2}}{|z_2|^2}$
- $|z| = |\bar{z}| = \sqrt{a^2 + b^2}$
- $\bar{\bar{z}} = z$
- $\overline{z_1 + z_2} = \bar{z_1} + \bar{z_2}$
- $\overline{z_1 \times z_2} = \bar{z_1} \times \bar{z_2}$

- $\overline{\left(\dfrac{z_1}{z_2}\right)} = \dfrac{\overline{z_1}}{\overline{z_2}}$ (assuming $z_2 \neq 0$)
- $\overline{z^n} = (\overline{z})^n$

Argument (Angle): The argument of a complex number $z = a + bi$ is the angle θ the number makes with the positive real axis in the complex plane, often expressed in radians.

The argument is denoted as $arg(z)$ and can be computed using: $\theta = arg(z) = \tan^{-1}\left(\dfrac{b}{a}\right)$

Properties of Argument:
- $arg(bi) = \dfrac{\pi}{2}$ (for a purely imaginary number)
- $arg(-bi) = -\dfrac{\pi}{2}$ (for a purely imaginary number)
- $arg(\bar{z}) = -arg(z)$
- $arg(z_1 \times z_2) = arg(z_1) + arg(z_2)$
- $arg\left(\dfrac{z_1}{z_2}\right) = arg(z_1) - arg(z_2)$
- $arg(z^n) = n \cdot arg(z)$

Polar Form: A complex number can be also expressed in polar form as: $z = r(\cos\theta + i\sin\theta) = re^{i\theta}$, where $r = |z|$ is the modulus and $\theta = arg(z)$ is the argument.

2.4.2. (Algebra) (Complex Numbers) Operations with Complex Numbers

Addition: Add real and imaginary parts separately.
$(a + bi) + (c + di) = (a + c) + (b + d)i$

Subtraction: Subtract real and imaginary parts separately:
$(a + bi) - (c + di) = (a - c) + (b - d)i$

Multiplication: Used the distributive property and the fact that $i^2 = -1$:
$(a + bi)(c + di) = (ac - bd) + (ad + bc)i$

Division: Multiply numerator and the denominator by the conjugate of the denominator:

PROBLEMS IN SCHOOL MATHEMATICS

$$\frac{a+bi}{c+di} = \frac{(a+bi)(c-di)}{(c+di)(c-di)} = \frac{(ac+bd)+(bc-ad)i}{c^2+d^2}$$

Feature	Real Number	Complex Number
Standard Form	a (where a is a real number)	$a + bi$ (where a and b are real numbers, and i is the imaginary unit)
Imaginary Part	Always 0 (there is no imaginary component)	May or may not have an imaginary part (non-zero b represents the imaginary parts)
Real Part	Non-zero or zero	Always present (could be zero or non-zero)
Graph Representation	Represented on a one dimensional number line (real axis)	Represented on a two-dimensional complex plane with real and imaginary axes

2.5. (Algebra) Linear Inequalities

Linear inequalities are mathematical expressions that involve linear functions and inequalities. They describe regions on a graph where the linear inequalities holds true. A linear inequality in two variables, such as $ax + by \leq c, ax + by \geq c, ax + by < c,$ or $ax + by > c$, represents a region of the coordinate plane that is bounded by a line. The inequality determines whether the region is above, below, or on one side of the line.

2.5.1. (Algebra) (Linear Inequalities) Addition and Subtraction

Equal numbers may be added to (or subtracted from) both sides of an inequality without affecting the sign of inequality.

2.5.2. (Algebra) (Linear Inequalities) Multiplication and Division

Both sides of an inequality can be multiplied (or divided) by the same positive number. But when both sides are multiplied or divided by a negative number, then the sign of inequality is reversed.

Feature	Linear Equalities	Linear Inequalities
Graphical Representation	A single point on a number line or a straight line on a coordinate plane	A shaded region or interval on a number line, or a half-plane on a coordinate plane
Solution	Gives a specific value of the variable	Gives a range of values for the variable

2.5.3. (Algebra) (Linear Inequalities) Properties of Linear Inequalities

> **Addition/Subtraction:** If $a < b$, then $a \pm c < b \pm c$
> **Multiplication/Division:**

If $a < b$, then $ac < bc$ (for $c > 0$)
If $a < b$, then $ac > bc$ (for $c < 0$)
If $a < b$, then $\dfrac{a}{c} < \dfrac{b}{c}$ (for $c > 0$)
If $a < b$, then $\dfrac{a}{c} > \dfrac{b}{c}$ (for $c < 0$)

> **Transitivity:** If $a < b$ and $b < c$, then $a < c$
> **Substitution:**

If $a = b$, replace a with b in any inequality

> **Addition/Subtraction of Inequalities:**

If $a < b$ and $c < d$, then $a \pm c < b \pm d$

> **Reversal:** $a < b$ becomes $b > a$

PROBLEMS IN SCHOOL MATHEMATICS

Interval	Interval Name	Real Number Line
$a < x < b$ or $x \in (a, b)$	Open Interval	
$a \leq x \leq b$ or $x \in [a, b]$	Closed Interval	
$a \leq x < b$ or $x \in [a, b)$	Closed-Open Interval	
$a < x \leq b$ or $x \in (a, b]$	Open-Closed Interval	

2.6. (Algebra) Permutations & Combinations
Permutations and combinations are fundamental concepts in combinatorics, a branch of mathematics concerned with counting and arrangements.

2.6.1. (Algebra) (Permutations & Combinations) Permutations
Permutations refer to the different ways of arranging a set of items where the order matters. For example, if three letters A, B and C, the permutations of these letters would include ABC, ACB, BAC, BCA, CAB and CBA. The formula to find the number of permutations of n distinct items is $n!$ (n factorial), where $n! = n \times (n-1) \times (n-2) \times ... \times 1$

2.6.2. (Algebra) (Permutations & Combinations) Combinations
Combinations refer to the different ways of selecting items from a set where the order does not selecting items from a set where the orders not matter. For example, if you want to choose 2 letters from A, B and C, the combinations are AB, AC and BC. The formula for combinations is $\binom{n}{k} = \frac{n!}{k!(n-k)!}$, where n is the total number of items, and k is the number of items to choose.

Feature	Permutations	Combinations
Formula	$P(n,r) = \dfrac{n!}{(n-r)!}$	$C(n,r) = \dfrac{n!}{r!(n-r)!}$
Key Concept	Focuses on how items are arranged or sequenced	Focuses on how items are grouped or selected
Real-world Example	Arranging people in a line, codes, schedules	Forming committees, selecting teams

2.7. (Algebra) Binomial Theorem

The binomial theorem provides a way to expand expression raised to a power. Specifically, it describes how to expand the expression $(a + b)^n$ where a and b are any numbers, and n is a non-negative integer.

The Binomial Theorem states that:

$$(a + b)^n = \sum_{k=0}^{n} \binom{n}{k} a^{n-k} b^k$$

Here's what each term represents:

$\binom{n}{k}$ is the binomial coefficient, also written as "n choose k", and represents the number of ways to choose k items from n items. It is calculate as $\dfrac{n!}{k!(n-k)!}$.

a^{n-k} is a raised to the power of $n - k$.

b^k is b raised to the power of k.

Properties of Binomial co-efficient:

- $\binom{n}{k} = \dfrac{n!}{k!(n-k)!}$
- $\binom{n}{k} \geq 0$ for $n \geq 0$ and $0 \leq k \leq n$
- $\binom{n}{k} = 0$ if $k < 0$ or $k > n$
- $\binom{n}{k} = \binom{n}{n-k}$

- $\binom{n}{k} = \binom{n-1}{k-1} + \binom{n-1}{k}$
- $\sum_{k=0}^{n} \binom{n}{k} = 2^n$
- $\binom{n}{k} = \frac{n(n-1)(n-2)\ldots(n-k+1)}{k!}$
- $\binom{n}{0} = 1$
- $\binom{n}{n} = 1$

Pascal's Triangle: Pascal's triangle is a triangular array of numbers where each entry is the sum of two numbers directly above it. The triangle starts with "1" at the top, and it continues downward with increasing rows.

Index	Coefficients
0	1
1	1 1
2	1 2 1
3	1 3 3 1
4	1 4 6 4 1
5	1 5 10 10 5 1

Each number in Pascal's triangle represents the binomial coefficients, which are used in binomial expansions.

2.8. (Algebra) Matrices & Determinants

Matrix: A matrix is a rectangular array of numbers or symbols arranged in rows and columns. It is fundamental concept in linear algebra and is used to represent linear transformations, solve systems of linear equations, and perform various operations in applied mathematics.

Determinant: A determinant is a scalar value that can be computed from a square matrix (i.e., a matrix same number of rows and columns). The determinant provides important properties about the matrix, such as whether it is invertible. For a 2 × 2 matrix

$$A = \begin{pmatrix} a & b \\ c & d \end{pmatrix}$$

The determinant is calculate as $det(A) = ad - bc$

2.8.1. (Algebra) (Matrices & Determinants) Types of Matrices

Square Matrix: Has the same number of rows and columns.
Rectangular Matrix: The number of rows and columns are different.
Diagonal Matrix: A square matrix where all off-diagonal elements are zero. Only the elements on the main diagonal (from top left to bottom right) may be non-zero.
Scalar Matrix: A diagonal matrix where all the diagonal elements are the same scalar value.
Identity Matrix: A diagonal matrix with all diagonal elements equal to 1. It acts as the multiplicative identity in matrix multiplication.
Zero Matrix: All elements are zero.
Symmetric Matrix: A square matrix is equal to its transpose $(i.e., A = A^T)$
Skew-Symmetric Matrix: A square matrix where the transpose is the negative of the matrix. $(i.e., A^T = -A)$
Upper Triangular Matrix: A square matrix where all elements below the main diagonal are zero.
Lower Triangular Matrix: A square matrix where all the elements above the main diagonal are zero.
Row Matrix: A matrix with a single row.
Column Matrix: A matrix with a single column.

2.8.2. (Algebra) (Matrices & Determinants) Operation on Matrices

Addition: A corresponding elements of two matrices. Matrices must be of the same dimensions. For matrices A and B:
$(A + B)_{ij} = A_{ij} + B_{ij}$

Subtraction: Subtract corresponding elements of two matrices. Matrices must be of the same dimensions. For matrices A and B:
$(A - B)_{ij} = A_{ij} - B_{ij}$

Scalar Multiplication: Multiply each element of a matrix by a scalar k.
$(kA)_{ij} = k.A_{ij}$

Matrix Multiplication: Multiply two matrices by taking dot product of rows and columns. For matrices A (of size $m \times n$) and B (of size $n \times p$)
$$(AB)_{ij} = \sum_{k=1}^{n} A_{ik}.B_{kj}$$

Transpose: Swap rows and columns of a matrix A.
$(A^T)_{ij} = A_{ji}$

Inverse: Find a matrix A^{-1} such that $AA^{-1} = I$ (the identity matrix). Only square matrices with a non-zero determinant have inverse.

Rank: Determine the maximum number of linearly independent rows and columns in a matrix, representing its dimensionality.

Elementary Operation on Matrices:
- **Row (or Column) Swapping:** This operation exchanges two rows (or two columns) of a matrix.
- **Row (or Column) Scaling:** This involves multiplying all elements of a row (or column) by a non-zero scalar.

PROBLEMS IN SCHOOL MATHEMATICS

> ➢ ***Row (or Column) Addition:*** *This operation adds a multiple of one row (or column) to another row (or column).*

2.9. (Algebra) Logarithm
A logarithm is a mathematical function that determines the exponent to which a base number must be raised to produce a given number. It is the inverse operation of exponentiation. The logarithm of a number x with base b is denoted as $\log_b(x)$ and is defined by the equation:
$b^y = x$ is equivalent to $y = \log_b(x)$
Where y is the logarithm of x with base b.

2.9.1. (Algebra) (Logarithm) Common types of Logarithm
Common Logarithm: Base 10, denoted as $\log(x)$ or $\log_{10}(x)$.
Natural Logarithm: Base e (approximately 2.718), denoted as $\ln(x)$.
Binary Logarithm: Base 2, denoted as $\log_2(x)$.

2.9.2. (Algebra) (Logarithm) Properties of Logarithms:
Product Rule: $\log_b(xy) = \log_b(x) + \log_b(y)$
Quotient Rule: $\log_b\left(\frac{x}{y}\right) = \log_b(x) - \log_b(y)$
Power Rule: $\log_b(x^k) = k \cdot \log_b(x)$
Change of Base Formula: $\log_b(x) = \frac{\log_k(x)}{\log_k(b)}$ for any positive value of k.
Logarithm of 1: $\log_b(1) = 0$
Logarithm of the Base: $\log_b(b) = 1$

2.10. (Algebra) Boolean Algebra

Boolean algebra is branch of algebra that deals with binary variables logical operations. It is fundamental to digital logic design and is used in areas such as computer science, electrical engineering, and mathematical logic. Boolean algebra operates with only two values, typically denoted as 1 (true) and 0 (false).

2.10.1. (Algebra) (Boolean Algebra) Basic Operations in Boolean Algebra

AND (Conjunction): The result is true if and only if both operands are true. It is denoted $A.B$ or simply AB.
$A \wedge B = 1$ if both $A = 1$ and $B = 1$

OR (Disjunction): The result is true if at least one of the operands is true. It is denoted as $A + B$.
$A \vee B = 1$ if either $A = 1$ or $B = 1$

Not (Negation or Complement): The result is the opposite of the operand.
If $A = 1$ then $\bar{A} = 0$, and if $A = 0$ then $\bar{A} = 1$

2.10.2. (Algebra) (Boolean Algebra) Laws of Boolean Algebra

Identity Law: $A + 0 = A$ & $A.1 = A$
Null Law: $A + 1 = 1$ & $A.0 = 0$
Idempotent Law: $A + A = A$ & $A.A = A$
Complement Law: $A + \bar{A} = 1$ & $A.\bar{A} = 0$
Distributive Law: $A.(B + C) = (A.B) + (A.C)$
$A + (B.C) = (A + B).(A + C)$
De Morgan's Theorems: $\overline{(A.B)} = \bar{A} + \bar{B}$ & $\overline{(A + B)} = \bar{A}.\bar{B}$
Double Negation Law: $\overline{(\bar{A})} = A$

PROBLEMS IN SCHOOL MATHEMATICS

2.10.3 (Algebra) (Boolean Algebra) Truth Tables

A	B	A∧B	A∨B
0	0	0	0
0	1	0	1
1	0	0	1
1	1	1	1

PROBLEMS IN SCHOOL MATHEMATICS

Problems

Algebra (Polynomial) 1
Simplify $m - 2n + \left[4n - \overline{3m - \{(1+2)m - 2n\}}\right]$.
Hint
$m - 2n + \left[4n - \overline{3m - \{(1+2)m - 2n\}}\right]$
$= m - 2n + [4n - 3m + \{(1+2)m - 2n\}]$

Algebra (Polynomial) 2
Divide $(x^4 - y^4)^2$ by $(x+y)$.
Hint
$x^4 - y^4 = (x^2 + y^2)(x+y)(x-y)$

Algebra (Polynomial) 3
Find the value of $\dfrac{a}{1 - \dfrac{1}{1 - \dfrac{1}{1 - \dfrac{1}{a}}}} \times \dfrac{b}{1 - \dfrac{1}{1 - \dfrac{1}{1 - \dfrac{1}{b}}}}$?

Hint
$$\dfrac{a}{1 - \dfrac{1}{1 - \dfrac{1}{1 - \dfrac{1}{a}}}} \times \dfrac{b}{1 - \dfrac{1}{1 - \dfrac{1}{1 - \dfrac{1}{b}}}}$$

$$= \dfrac{a}{1 - \dfrac{1}{1 - 1 \times \dfrac{a}{a-1}}} \times \dfrac{b}{1 - \dfrac{1}{1 - 1 \times \dfrac{b}{b-1}}}$$

Algebra (Polynomial) 4
If $a=1$, $b=2$, $c=3$ and $d=4$, find the value of
$\dfrac{2\sqrt{ab^2c^2d} + 3\sqrt{a^3b^4c^4d^3}}{4\sqrt[3]{a^6b^6c^9d^{12}}}$?

Hint

$$\frac{2\sqrt{ab^2c^2d} + 3\sqrt{a^3b^4c^4d^3}}{4\sqrt[3]{a^6b^6c^9d^{12}}}$$

$$=\frac{2(ab^2c^2d)^{\frac{1}{2}} + 3(a^3b^4c^4d^3)^{\frac{1}{2}}}{4(a^6b^6c^9d^{12})^{\frac{1}{3}}}$$

Algebra (Polynomial) 5

Find the value of $\dfrac{abc}{\sqrt{\dfrac{1}{a^{-2}}\sqrt{\dfrac{1}{b^{-4}}\sqrt{\dfrac{1}{c^{-16}}}}}} = ?$

Hint

$$\sqrt{\dfrac{1}{a^{-2}}\sqrt{\dfrac{1}{b^{-4}}\sqrt{\dfrac{1}{c^{-16}}}}} = abc$$

Algebra (Polynomial) 6

If $\dfrac{\sqrt{7+x} + \sqrt{7-x}}{\sqrt{7+x} - \sqrt{7-x}} = 5$, then find the value of x?

Hint

$\dfrac{\sqrt{7+x} + \sqrt{7-x}}{\sqrt{7+x} - \sqrt{7-x}} = 5$

Or, $\sqrt{7+x} + \sqrt{7-x} = 5\sqrt{7+x} - 5\sqrt{7-x}$

Or, $6\sqrt{7-x} = 4\sqrt{7+x}$

(Square both sides of the equation)

Algebra (Polynomial) 7

Reduce to lowest terms $\dfrac{x^3 + x^2 - 37x + 35}{x^3 + 5x^2 - 29x - 105}$.

PROBLEMS IN SCHOOL MATHEMATICS

Hint
$(x-5)$ and $(x+7)$ are factors of
$(x^3 + x^2 - 37x + 35)$ and $(x^3 + 5x^2 - 29x - 105)$ respectively.

Algebra (Polynomial) 8
Find the square roots of $11a + 2a\sqrt{30}$?
Hint
$11a + 2a\sqrt{30}$
$= (\sqrt{5a})^2 + (\sqrt{6a})^2 + 2 \times \sqrt{5a} \times \sqrt{6a}$
$= (\sqrt{5a} + \sqrt{6a})^2$

Algebra (Polynomial) 9
Factorize $x^3 - 9x^2 - 129x + 1001$.
Hint
$(x-7)$ is the factor of $(x^3 - 9x^2 - 129x + 1001)$

Algebra (Polynomial) 10
Factorize $a^2b - 2ab + b + a^2c - 2ac + c$.
Hint
$(b+c)$ is the factor of $(a^2b - 2ab + b + a^2c - 2ac + c)$

Algebra (Polynomial) 11
Factorize $x^{16} + x^8 + 1$.
Hint
$x^{16} + x^8 + 1 = x^{16} + 2x^8 + 1 - x^8$
$= (x^8)^2 + 2 \times x^8 \times 1 + (1)^2 - (x^4)^2$

PROBLEMS IN SCHOOL MATHEMATICS

Algebra (Polynomial) 12
If x, y and z are all non-zeros and $x + y + z = 0$, then prove that $\frac{x^2}{yz} + \frac{y^2}{zx} + \frac{z^2}{xy} = 3$.

Hint
$x^3 + y^3 + z^3 - 3xyz$
$= (x + y + z)(x^2 + y^2 + z^2 - xy - yz - zx)$

Algebra (Polynomial) 13
If α and β are the zeros of the polynomial $x^2 - ax + b$, then find the value of $\frac{(\alpha-\beta)^3}{\alpha\beta} + \frac{\alpha}{\beta} + \frac{\beta}{\alpha} + 1$?

Hint
$$\frac{(\alpha-\beta)^3}{\alpha\beta} + \frac{\alpha}{\beta} + \frac{\beta}{\alpha} + 1$$
$$= \frac{\left[\pm\sqrt{(\alpha+\beta)^2 - 4\alpha\beta}\right]^3 + \alpha^2 + \beta^2 + \alpha\beta}{\alpha\beta}$$
$$= \frac{\left[\pm\sqrt{(\alpha+\beta)^2 - 4\alpha\beta}\right]^3 + (\alpha+\beta)^2 - \alpha\beta}{\alpha\beta}$$

Where $\alpha + \beta = -\frac{\text{coefficient of } x}{\text{coefficient of } x^2}$

And $\alpha\beta = \frac{\text{constant term}}{\text{coefficient of } x^2}$

Algebra (Polynomial) 14
Solve $3x^2 - 5x - 8 = 0$.

Hint
Use quadratic formula $x = \frac{-b \pm \sqrt{b^2 - 4ac}}{2a}$

Algebra (Polynomial) 15
If $\frac{p}{x} + \frac{q}{y} = m$ and $\frac{q}{x} + \frac{p}{y} = n$, then find the value of $\frac{x}{y}$?
Hint
Let $\frac{1}{x} = u$ and $\frac{1}{y} = v$

Algebra (Polynomial) 16
If 2 bags together with 4 boxes weigh 'a' kg 'b' gm and 3 bags together with 3 boxes weigh 'a' kg 'c' gm, find the weight of each bag and box.
Hint
Let weight of each bag and each box be 'x' gm and 'y' gm respectively.
$2x + 4y = (a \times 1000) + b$
$3x + 3y = (a \times 1000) + c$

Algebra (Polynomial) 17
Three candidates Rudrajit, Debdas and Paribrita participated in an election. Rudrajit gets 40% of votes more than Debdas. Paribrita gets 20% votes more than Debdas. Rudrajit also overtakes Paribrita by 10000 votes. If 90% voters voted and no invalid or illegal votes were cast, then what will be the number of voters in the voting list?

Hint
Let the number of votes casted for Debdas be x
Votes casted for Rudrajit $= x + 40\%$ of $x = 1.4x$
Votes casted for Paribrita $= x + 20\%$ of $x = 1.2x$

Algebra (Polynomial) 18
Uttarayan having sold at Rs 75 a drawing which cost him Rs S, finds that he has realized S% profit on his outlay. Find the value of S?

Hint
$S \times S\% = (75 - S)$

Algebra (Polynomial) 19
Two entrepreneurs Bhargav and Sahin have 15 apparatus between them; they sell them at different prices, but each receives the same sum. If Bhargav sold his at Sahin price, he would have received Rs 245000; and if Sahin had sold his at Bhargav's price, he would have received Rs 320000. How many had each?

Hint
Let Bhargav have x and Sahin have y number of apparatus, they sell them at Rs 'a' and Rs 'b' respectively.
Therefore $x + y = 15$ and $ax = by$
But, $\dfrac{bx}{ay} = \dfrac{245000}{320000}$
Or, $\dfrac{x^2}{y^2} = \dfrac{49}{64}$

Algebra (Polynomial) 20

Kumkum, Bhaswati and Bristi started a business together. The respective ratio of investments of Kumkum and Bhaswati was 3:5 and the respective ratio of investments

of Bhaswati and Bristi was 10:13. If at the end of the year, Bristi received Rs 5876 as her share of annual profit, what was total annual profit earned by all of them together?

Hint

Kumkum:Bhaswati:Bristi = 6:10:13

Algebra (Polynomial) 21

Sagnik borrowed Rs 800 at 6% and Diptanu borrowed Rs 600 at 10%. After how much time, will they both have equal debts?

Hint

Let after 't' years they both have equal debts

$\therefore 800 + \frac{800 \times 6 \times t}{100} = 600 + \frac{600 \times 10 \times t}{100}$

Algebra (Polynmial) 22

Two ladies Subhrasmita and Sourasmita start simultaneously from two places, 'd' kilometers apart, and walk in the same direction. Subhrasmita travels of the rate of 'm' kilometers per hour, and Sourasmita at the rate of 'n' kilometers; how far will Subhrasmita have walked before she over takes Sourasmita?

Hint

Let Subhrasmita walked 'x' kilometers when she overtakes Sourasmita, Sourasmita walked '(x-d)' kilometers.

Subhrasmita's time = Sourasmita's time

Or, $\frac{x}{m} = \frac{x-d}{n}$

Algebra (Polynomial) 23

The speed of Sanjoy's car is $\frac{6}{5}$ speed of Pritam's car. These cover the distance of 100 km from Agartala to Sabroom in the same time, while Sanjoy's car stops for 10 minutes on the way for refueling. What is the speed of Pritam's car?

Hint

Let the speed of Pritam's car be 'x' km/h

Speed of Sanjoy's car is $\frac{6x}{5}$ km/h

PROBLEMS IN SCHOOL MATHEMATICS

$Time = \dfrac{Distance}{Speed}$

$\therefore \dfrac{100}{x} - \dfrac{100}{\frac{6x}{5}} = \dfrac{10}{60}$

Algebra (Polynomial) 24
Two boys Sahil and Arijit run 4 km race on a course 0.25 km round. If their speeds are in the ratio 5:4, how often winner pass the another?

Hint
Let Sahil will overtake Arijit when he complete 5 rounds.
Distance travelled by Sahil,
when crossing Arijit = 5×0.25 = 1.25 km
Therefore, Sahil will pass Arijit = $\dfrac{4}{1.25}$ times

Algebra (Polynomial) 25
Subhrajit, Soumyarup and Samarjit walk 1 km in 5 minutes, 8 minutes and 10 minutes respectively. Samarjit starts walking from a point at a certain time, Soumyarup starts from the same point 1 minutes later and Subhrajit starts from the same point 2 minutes later than Samarjit. Then find the times Subhrajit meet Samarjit and Soumyarup?

Hint
Let Subhrajit meets Soumyarup and Samarjit in 'x' and 'y' minutes respectively.
Distance covered by Soumyarup in '$(x + 1)$' minutes equal to distance covered by Subhrajit in 'x' minutes

Distance covered by Samarjit in '(y + 2)' minutes equal to distance covered by Subhrajit in 'y' minutes

Algebra (Polynomial) 26
Bishwajit can row 6 km/h in still water. If the speed of the current is 2 km/h, it takes 3 hours more in upstream than in the downstream for the same distance. Find the distance?

Hint
Let the total distance be 'x' km

$\therefore \dfrac{x}{6-2} - \dfrac{x}{6+2} = 3$

Algebra (Polynomial) 27
A ferry is moving downstream from city Amarpur to city Udaipur with speed 45 km/h, Diksit jumped into the river in middle of cities and starts swimming toward Amarpur. Ferry reached Udaipur and comes to Amarpur with speed 30 km/h and both reached at the same time.

What is the speed of Diksit in river?

Hint
Let the speed of ferry be 'x' km/h and speed of current be 'y' km/h

$x + y = 45$ and $x - y = 30$

Therefore, $x = \frac{75}{2}$ and $y = \frac{15}{2}$

Suppose the speed of Diksit be 'a' km/h and distance between two cities be 'd' km

$$\therefore \frac{\frac{d}{2}}{x+y} + \frac{d}{x-y} = \frac{\frac{d}{2}}{a-y}$$

Algebra (Polynomial) 28
How many men will be required to do in 'x' hours, what 'y' men do in 'nx' hours?

Hint
'x' hours is the time required by $\frac{y \times nx}{x}$ men

Algebra (Polynomial) 29
The Efficiency of Bhumika is twice that of Snigdha, whereas the efficiency of Bhumika and Snigdha together is three times that of Piyali. If Bhumika, Snigdha and Piyali worked together on a job, in what ratio should they share their earnings?

Hint
Let time taken by Bhumika and Snigdha to complete the work be 'x' days and '2x' days respectively.

Bhumika and Snigdha's one day work $= \frac{1}{x} + \frac{1}{2x} = \frac{3}{2x}$

Piyali's will complete the work =
$3 \times$ *Bhumika and Snigdha's whole work in days*

$$= 3 \times \frac{2x}{3} = 2x$$

Therefore, Piyali's one day work $= \frac{1}{2x}$

Algebra (Polynomial) 30

Arnab and Aryaan attempted to solve a quadratic equation. Arnab made a mistake in writing down the constant term ending up in roots (4,3). Aryaan made a mistake in writing down the coefficient of x to get roots (3,2). Find the correct roots of the equation?

Hint

First Condition

$4 + 3 = -\frac{coefficient\ of\ x}{coefficient\ of\ x^2}$

$4 \times 3 = \frac{constant\ term}{coefficient\ of\ x^2}$

Second Condition

$3 + 2 = -\frac{coefficient\ of\ x}{coefficient\ of\ x^2}$

$3 \times 2 = \frac{constant\ term}{coefficient\ of\ x^2}$

Algebra (Sets) 31

Write the set $\left\{1, \frac{3}{7}, \frac{1}{6}, \frac{3}{49}\right\}$ in set-builder form.

Hint

$\frac{1+2+3}{1^n+2^n+3^n}$, where n is a natural number and $n \leq 4$

Algebra (Sets) 32

Draw the Venn diagram $(A - B) \cup (B - C) \cup (C - A)$.

Hint

$(A - B) \cup (B - C) \cup (C - A) = A \cup B \cup C$

Algebra (Sets) 33

If $B \subset A$ and $D \subset C$ and $A \cap C \neq \emptyset$ and

$(A \cap B) \cap (C \cap D) = \emptyset$, then prove that $B \cap D = \emptyset$.
Hint

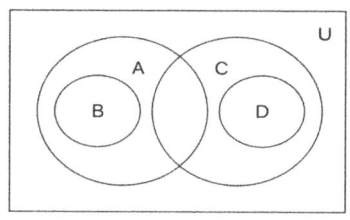

Algebra (Sets) 34
If $A \subset B$ and $B \subset C$ then,
prove that $(A \cap B \cap C) \cup (A' \cap B' \cap C') = \emptyset$.
Hint
$A \cap B \cap C = A$ and $A' \cap B' \cap C' = C'$

Algebra (Sets) 35
If $A \cap B = \emptyset$ and $(A \cup C) \cap (B \cup C) = C$, then
prove that $(A \cup C) \cap (B \cup C) = (C - A) \cup (C - B)$.
Hint

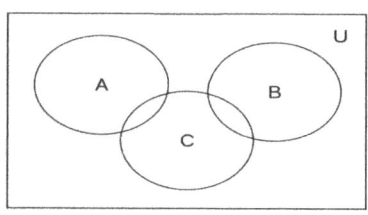

Algebra (Relations & Functions) 36
If $A \cap B \cap C = \emptyset$, then
prove that $(A \times B) \cap (B \times C) \cap (C \times A) = \emptyset$.

PROBLEMS IN SCHOOL MATHEMATICS

Hint
Let $A = \{a, b\}$, $B = \{c, d\}$, $C = \{e, f\}$

Algebra (Relations & Functions) 37
If $pf(x) + qf\left(\frac{1}{x}\right) = +1$, where $p \neq q$ and $x \neq -1$, then find $f(x)$?
Hint
$pf(x) + qf\left(\frac{1}{x}\right) = x + 1$ and $pf\left(\frac{1}{x}\right) + qf(x) = \frac{1}{x+1}$

Algebra (Relations & Functions) 38
Find the domain and range of the real function
$f(x) = \frac{x+5}{x^2+11x+30}$?
Hint
$\frac{x+5}{x^2+11x+30} = \frac{x+5}{(x+5)(x+6)}$

Algebra (Relations & Functions) 39
Find the domain and range of the real function
$f(x) = \sqrt{\frac{x^3-23x^2+142x-120}{(x-10)(x-12)}}$?
Hint
$x^3 - 23x^2 + 142x - 120 = (x-1)(x-10)(x-12)$

Algebra (Relations & Functions) 40
Let $f = \left\{\left(x, \sqrt{\frac{x-|x|}{x+|x|}}\right) : x \in R\right\}$ be a function from R into R.
Determine the range of f?

PROBLEMS IN SCHOOL MATHEMATICS

Hint

$\frac{x-|x|}{x+|x|} \geq 0$ and $x - |x| < x + |x|$

Algebra (Complex Numbers) 41

Write the complex number in $a + ib$ form

$\left[\frac{25(-1+7i)}{24(7+i)}\right]^{1000}.$

Hint

$\left[\frac{25(-1+7i)}{24(7+i)}\right]^{1000} = \left[\frac{25(-1+7i)(7-i)}{24(7+i)(7-i)}\right]^{1000}$

Algebra (Complex Numbers) 42

Evaluate $\left[i^{99} + \frac{1}{i^{99}}\right]^3.$

Hint

$\left[i^{99} + \frac{1}{i^{99}}\right]^3 = \left[(i^3)^{33} + \frac{i}{(i^2)^{50}}\right]^3$

Algebra (Complex Numbers) 43

For all complex numbers z_1 and z_2, prove that
$|z_1 z_2| = |z_1||z_2|$ and $\left|\frac{z_1}{z_2}\right| = \frac{|z_1|}{|z_2|}, z_2 \neq 0.$

Hint

Let $z_1 = a + ib$ and $z_2 = c + id$
$z_1 z_2 = (ac - bd) + i(ad + bc)$
$\frac{z_1}{z_2} = \frac{(ac+bd)+i(bc-ad)}{(c^2+d^2)}$

Algebra (Complex Numbers) 44

Find the complex number z, satisfying the equation

$2z + |z||\bar{z}| + 2i = 0$?

Hint

Let complex number, $z = a + ib$

$\bar{z} = a - ib$

$\therefore |z| = \sqrt{a^2 + b^2}$ and $|\bar{z}| = \sqrt{a^2 + b^2}$

Algebra (Complex Numbers) 45

Let z_1 and z_2 be two complex numbers such that
$z_1|z_1 - z_2|^2 - z_2|\overline{z_1} - \overline{z_2}|^2 = n(z_1 - z_2)^2(\overline{z_1} - \overline{z_2})$. Find the value of n?

Hint

$z_1|z_1 - z_2|^2 - z_2|\overline{z_1} - \overline{z_2}|^2$
$= z_1(z_1 - z_2)(\overline{z_1 - z_2}) - z_2(\overline{z_1 - z_2})(z_1 - z_2)$
$= z_1(z_1 - z_2)(\overline{z_1} - \overline{z_2}) - z_2(\overline{z_1} - \overline{z_2})(z_1 - z_2)$

Algebra (Linear Inequalities) 46

Solve $(x + 5)^3 - (x - 2)^3 \geq 91$ for real x.

Hint

$(x + 5)^3 - (x - 2)^3 \geq 91$

Or,

$x^3 + 15x^2 + 75x + 125 - x^3 + 6x^2 - 12x + 8 - 91 \geq 0$

Algebra (Linear Inequalities) 47

Find the real values of x, for which $\sqrt{\frac{(x+3)(x-7)}{(x-10)}}$ takes real values?

Hint

$\frac{(x+3)(x+7)}{(x-10)} \geq 0$ and $x - 10 \neq 0$

PROBLEMS IN SCHOOL MATHEMATICS

Algebra (Linear Inequalities) 48
Show that $(x + y + z)^3 > 3xyz$.
Hint
$(x + y + z)^3 = x^3 + y^3 + z^3 + 3(x + y)(y + z)(z + x)$

Algebra (Linear Inequalities) 49
A solution of 10% H_2SO_4 is to be diluted by adding a 4% H_2SO_4 acid solution to it. The resulting mixture is to be more than 6% but less than 8% H_2SO_4. If there are 500 litres of the 4% solution, then how many litres of 10% solution is.
Hint
Let x litres of 10% solution
6% of $(x + 500) < 10\%$ of $x + 4\%$ of $500 < 8\%$ of $(x + 500)$

Algebra (Linear Inequalities) 50
Men with a medium body frame, the ideal weight ranges from 50 to 73 kg for heights between 5′4″ to 6′0″. What is the range of weight in pound (lb) and range of heights in centimeter? If the conversion formula is 1 kg = 2.2 lb and 1 inch = $\frac{1}{2.54}$ cm.
Hint
$50 < 2.2 \, lb < 73$ and
$(5 \times 12 + 4) < \frac{1}{2.54} \, cm < (6 \times 12 + 0)$

Algebra (Permutations & Combinations) 51
How many classifications are there for a deck of 52 cards, if all the cards of same color are together?

PROBLEMS IN SCHOOL MATHEMATICS

Hint
$2!\,(26!)^2$

Algebra (Permutations & Combinations) 52
Pranaya has three pockets and ten chocolates. In how many ways can she put the chocolates in her pockets?

Hint
Total number of ways $= 3^{10}$

Algebra (Permutations & Combinations) 53
In how many ways can the letters of the longest English word Pneumonoultramicroscopicsilicovolcanoconiosis be arranged?
Hint
Total letters $= 45$
P- 2 times, N- 4 times, U- 2 times, M- 2 times, O- 9 times, L- 3 times, R- 2 times, A- 2 times, I- 6 times, C- 6 times, S- 4 times, E- 1 time, T- 1 time, V- 1 time

∴ Total number of ways $= \dfrac{45!}{2!\,4!\,2!\,2!\,9!\,3!\,2!\,2!\,6!\,6!\,4!\,1!\,1!\,1!}$

Algebra (Permutations & Combinations) 54
There are 100 candidates for an examination out of which 30 are appearing in Mathematics remaining 70 are appearing in Biology, out of which 10 and 40 candidates are girls in Mathematics and Biology respectively. In how many ways can they be seated in a row so that no two Biology boys are together?

PROBLEMS IN SCHOOL MATHEMATICS

Hint
Places available for Biology boys $= (100 - 30) + 1 = 71$
Therefore, total number of ways $= 70! \times {}^{71}P_{30}$

Algebra (Permutations & Combinations) 55
How many words can be made of English alphabet each containing 3 consonants and 2 vowels with or without meaning?
Hint
Total alphabet $= 26$
Consonants $= 21$ and vowels $= 5$
Therefore, the required number of words $= {}^{21}C_3 \times {}^{5}C_2 \times 5!$

Algebra (Permutations & Combinations) 56

In IPL, 45 matches were played. Every two teams played one match each other. Find the total number of teams?
Hint
Let total numbers of team be n
${}^nC_2 = 45$

Algebra (Permutations & Combinations) 57
The interior angles of a regular polygon measure $170°$ each. Then find the number of diagonals of the polygon?
Hint
Each exterior angle $= 180° - 170° = 10°$

Number of sides $= \dfrac{360° \times \frac{\pi}{180°}}{10° \times \frac{\pi}{180°}} = 36$

So, number of diagonals $= {}^{36}C_2 - 36$

Algebra (Permutations & Combination) 58
In how many sitting arrangements are possible if 35 boys and 15 girls be seated for picnic tour in two buses, having 20 and 30 numbered seats respectively, so that all girls are in same bus?

Hint
Condition One (All girls in first bus)
First Bus
${}^{15}C_{15} \times {}^{35}C_5$
Second Bus
${}^{35}C_{30}$
Condition Two (All girls in second bus)
First Bus
${}^{35}C_{20}$
Second Bus
${}^{35}C_{15} \times {}^{15}C_{15}$

Therefore, total number of seating arrangements =
${}^{15}C_{15} \times 15! \times {}^{35}C_5 \times 5! \times {}^{35}C_{30} \times 30! + {}^{35}C_{20} \times 20! \times {}^{35}C_{15} \times 15! \times {}^{15}C_{15} \times 15!$

Algebra (Permutations & Combinations) 59
From a class of 60 students divided into three groups; 'Group A', 'Group B' and 'Group C' containing 30, 20 and 10 students respectively. 15 students are to be chosen for an educational tour. There are 5 students (Binit, Raja, Anik, SaifUddin, Sujan) from 'Group A' who decide that

either all of them will join or none of them will join. In how many ways can the education tour be chosen, if at least 2 students from 'Group C'.

Hint
If 5 students will join $^{55}C_8 \times {}^{10}C_2 + {}^{55}C_0 \times {}^{10}C_{10}$
If 5 students will not join $^{55}C_{13} \times {}^{10}C_2 + {}^{55}C_5 \times {}^{10}C_{10}$
Therefore, total number of ways =
$^{55}C_8 \times {}^{10}C_2 + {}^{55}C_0 \times {}^{10}C_{10} + {}^{55}C_{13} \times {}^{10}C_2 + {}^{55}C_5 \times {}^{10}C_{10}$

Algebra (Permutations & Combinations) 60

12 family members are to be seated of a rectangular shape table for dinner, 4 members each on longer sides of a table and 2 members each on shorter sides of table. Two sisters Manisha and Ishita desire to sit on shorter side with other sisters Puja and Pio respectively, and three other members (Gopal, Soma & Aru) on one particular side. Find the number of ways in which the seating arrangements can be made?

Hint
Manisha and Puja on one shorter side $^4C_2$
Ishita and Pio on other shorter side $^{4-2}C_2 = {}^2C_2$
On longer side $^{12-4-3}C_4 = {}^5C_4$ and $^{5-4}C_1 = {}^1C_1$

Therefore, total arrangements =
$^4C_2 \times 2! \times {^2C_2} \times 2! \times {^5C_4} \times 4! \times {^1C_1} \times 4!$

Algebra (Binomial Theorem) 61
Find the expansion of $(m + n - 1)^{10}$.
Hint
$(m + n - 1)^{10} =$
$^{10}C_0(m)^{10} + {^{10}C_1}(m)^9(n-1)^1 \ldots \ldots \ldots \ldots \ldots + {^{10}C_{10}}(n-1)^{10}$

Algebra (Binomial Theorem) 62
Find the coefficient of $\frac{1}{x^{118}}$ in the expansion of $\left(x^7 - \frac{1}{x^{11}}\right)^{500}$.
Hint
$T_{r+1} = {^{500}C_r}(x^7)^{500-r}\left(-\frac{1}{x^{11}}\right)^r$

Algebra (Binomial Theorem) 63
Find the middle term of $\left(x + \frac{1}{x}\right)^{100n}$.
Hint
Middle term $= \left(\frac{100n}{2} + 1\right)$th term $=$
$^{100n}C_{50n}(x)^{100n-50n}\left(\frac{1}{x}\right)^{50n}$

Algebra (Binomial Theorem) 64
Find the greatest term in the expansion of $(a + b)^{12}$ when $a = 1$ and $b = 2$?

PROBLEMS IN SCHOOL MATHEMATICS

Hint

$T_{r+1} \geq T_r$

Algebra (Binomial Theorem) 65

Find the (a+1) th term from the end in $\left(x - \dfrac{1}{x}\right)^{2n+1}$.

Hint

$T_{a+1} = {}^{2n+1}C_a \left(-\dfrac{1}{x}\right)^{2n+1-a} (x)^a$

Algebra (Matrices and Determinants) 66

If $A = \begin{bmatrix} \sin\theta & \cos\theta \\ -\cos\theta & \sin\theta \end{bmatrix}$, verify that $AA' = I$, where I is the unit matrix.

Hint

$A' = \begin{bmatrix} \sin\theta & -\cos\theta \\ \cos\theta & \sin\theta \end{bmatrix}$

Algebra (Matrices & Determinants) 67

If $\begin{bmatrix} a & 0 \\ 1 & b \end{bmatrix}$ is a skew-symmetric matrix, then find the values of 'a' and 'b'.

Hint

$\begin{bmatrix} a & 1 \\ 0 & b \end{bmatrix} = -\begin{bmatrix} a & 0 \\ 1 & b \end{bmatrix}$

Algebra (Matrices and Determinants) 68

If $A = \begin{bmatrix} 0 & b \\ a & 0 \end{bmatrix}$, then find A^2?

Hint

$A^2 = A.A = \begin{bmatrix} 0 & b \\ a & 0 \end{bmatrix} \begin{bmatrix} 0 & b \\ a & 0 \end{bmatrix}$

PROBLEMS IN SCHOOL MATHEMATICS

Algebra (Matrices & Determinants) 69

If $x + y \neq 0$ and $\begin{vmatrix} x & y \\ y & x \end{vmatrix} = 0$, then prove that $x=y$.

Hint

$R_1' = R_1 + R_2$

Algebra (Matrices and Determinants) 70

Show that $\begin{vmatrix} a+1 & 1 \\ 1 & b+1 \end{vmatrix} = ab\left(1 + \frac{1}{a} + \frac{1}{b}\right)$.

Hint

Taking a and b common from R_1 and R_2

$ab \begin{vmatrix} 1+a^{-1} & a^{-1} \\ b^{-1} & 1+b^{-1} \end{vmatrix}$

Then apply $R_1' = R_1 + R_2$

Algebra (Logarithm) 71

Find the logarithm of $243\sqrt[5]{9}$ to base $3\sqrt{3}$.

Hint

$(3\sqrt{3})^x = 243\sqrt[5]{9}$

Or, $\left(3 \cdot 3^{\frac{1}{2}}\right)^x = 3^5 \cdot 3^{\frac{2}{5}}$

Or, $\left(3^{1+\frac{1}{2}}\right)^x = 3^{5+\frac{2}{5}}$

$\therefore \dfrac{3x}{2} = \dfrac{27}{5}$

Algebra (Logarithm) 72

Express the logarithm of $\dfrac{\sqrt{x^5}}{y^2 z^3}$ in terms of $\log x$, $\log y$ and $\log z$.

Hint

$$\log \frac{\sqrt{x^5}}{y^2 z^3} = \log \sqrt{x^5} - \log(y^2 z^3)$$
$$= \log x^{\frac{5}{2}} - \log(y^2 + z^3) = \frac{5}{2} \log x - 2 \log y - 3 \log z$$

Algebra (Logarithm) 73
Solve $\log(90000x + 10000) = 5$

Hint

$\log_{10}(90000x + 10000) = 5$
$Or, 90000x + 10000 = 10^5$
$\therefore x = \dfrac{100000 - 10000}{90000}$

Algebra (Logarithm) 74
Find the value of x from the equation
$$\log_3 \frac{x}{\sqrt{x}} = \frac{4}{\log_3 \frac{x}{\sqrt{x}}}$$

Hint

$\log_3 \sqrt{x} = \dfrac{4}{\log_3 \sqrt{x}}$

$Or, \dfrac{1}{2} \log_3 x = \dfrac{4}{\frac{1}{2} \log_3 x}$

$Or, \dfrac{1}{2} (\log_3 x)^2 = 2 \times 4$

$Or, (\log_3 x)^2 = 16$

$Or, \log_3 x = \pm 4$

$\therefore x = 3^4 \text{ or } 3^{-4}$

PROBLEMS IN SCHOOL MATHEMATICS

Algebra (Logarithm) 75
Find three places of decimals the value of x from the equation, $4^{x+3}.6^{7-2x}.9^{x-5} = 36$
(Given $\log 2 = 0.301$ and $\log 3 = 0.477$)

Hint

Taking logarithms of both sides, we have
$(x+3)\log 2^2 + (7-2x)\log(2.3) + (x-5)\log 3^2 = \log(2.3)^2$

Algebra (Boolean Algebra) 76
Prove that $(\overline{A.B.C}) + (\overline{\bar{A}.\bar{B}.\bar{C}}) = 1$

Hint

$\bar{A} + \bar{B} + \bar{C} + \bar{\bar{A}} + \bar{\bar{B}} + \bar{\bar{C}}$ *(De Morgan's Theorems)*
$= \bar{A} + \bar{B} + \bar{C} + A + B + C$ *(Double Negation Law)*
$= (A + \bar{A}) + (B + \bar{B}) + (C + \bar{C})$
$= 1 + 1 + 1$ *(Complement Law)*
$= 1$ *(True or true or true is true)*

Algebra (Boolean Algebra) 77
Solve $[(\overline{A.\bar{A}}).(\overline{B.\bar{B}})] + [(\overline{A+\bar{A}}).(\overline{B+\bar{B}})]$

Hint

$[(\overline{A.\bar{A}}).(\overline{B.\bar{B}})] + [(\overline{A+\bar{A}}).(\overline{B+\bar{B}})]$
$= [(\bar{0}).(\bar{0})] + [(\bar{1}).(\bar{1})]$ *(Complement Law)*
$= (1.1) + (0.0)$
$= 1 + 0$
$= 1$ *(Null Law)*

Algebra (Boolean Algebra) 78
Prove that $A.(A + \bar{A} + B + \bar{B}) = A$

PROBLEMS IN SCHOOL MATHEMATICS

Hint

$(A.A) + (A.\bar{A}) + (A.B) + (A.\bar{B})$ *(Distributive Law)*
$= A + 0 + A.B + A.\bar{B}$ *(Idempotent & Complement Law)*
$= A + A.(B + \bar{B})$ *(Distributive Law)*
$= A + A$ *(Complement Law)*
$= A$ *(Idempotent Law)*

Algebra (Boolean Algebra) 79

Simplify $(A + \bar{B})(\bar{A} + B)(A + B)$

Hint

$= (A\bar{A} + AB + \overline{BA} + \bar{B}B)(A + B)$ *(Distributive Law)*
$= (0 + AB + \overline{BA} + 0)(A + B)$ *(Complement Law)*
$= ABA + ABB + \overline{BA}(A + B)$ *(Distributive Law)*
$= (AB + AB) + (\bar{B} + \bar{A})(A + B)$
(Idempotent Law & De Morgan's Theorems)
$= AB + \bar{B}A + \bar{B}B + \bar{A}A + \bar{A}B$ *(Distributive Law)*
$= AB + \bar{B}A + 0 + 0 + \bar{A}B$ *(Complement Law)*
$= AB + \bar{B}A + \bar{A}B$
$= AB + A \oplus B$

Algebra (Boolean Algebra) 80

Minimize the expression $A\bar{B} + AB + \overline{AB} + AC$

Hint

$= A(\bar{B} + B) + \overline{AB} + AC$ *(Distributive Law)*
$= A.1 + AC + \overline{AB}$ *(Complement Law)*
$= A(1 + C) + \overline{AB}$ *(Distributive Law)*
$= A + \bar{A} + \bar{B}$ *(Null Law & De Morgan's Theorems)*
$= 1 + \bar{B}$ *(Complement Law)*

PROBLEMS IN SCHOOL MATHEMATICS

GEOMETRY

3. Geometry
Geometry is a branch of mathematics that studies the properties, measurements, and relationships of points, lines, surfaces, and solids in space.

3.1. (Geometry) Euclid's Axioms & Postulates
<u>Axioms (or Common Notions):</u>
  I. Things which are equal to the same thing are also equal to one another.
  II. If equals are added to equals, the wholes are equal.
  III. If equals are subtracted from equals, the remainders are equal.
  IV. Things which coincide with one another are equal to one another.
  V. The whole is greater than the part.
  VI. Things which are double of the same things are equal to one another.
  VII. Things which are halves of the same things are equal to one another.

<u>Postulates:</u>
  I. A straight line can be drawn from any point to any other point.
  II. A finite straight line can be extended continuously in a straight line.
  III. A circle can be drawn with any center and any radius.

IV. *All right angles are equal.*
V. *If a straight line falling on two straight lines makes the interior angles on the same side less than two right angles, then the two straight lines, if extended indefinitely, meet on that side on which the angles less than two right angles.*

3.2. (Geometry) Lines & Angles
Lines:
Line: *A straight path extending infinitely in both directions, with no curvatures.*
Line Segment: *A part of a line is bounded by two endpoints.*
Ray: *A line with a starting point that extends infinitely in one direction.*
Parallel Lines: *Lines are in the same plane that never intersects, no matter how far they are extended.*
Perpendicular Lines: *Lines that intersect at a right angle (90 degrees).*
Angles:
Angle: *Formed by two rays on line segments that share a common endpoint, called the vertex. The amount of turn between the two rays is measured in degrees.*
Types of Angles:
Acute Angle: *Less than 90 degrees.*
Right Angle: *Exactly 90 degrees.*
Obtuse Angle: *Greater than 90 degrees but less than 180 degrees.*
Straight Angle: *Exactly 180 degrees.*

Reflex Angle: *Greater than 180 degrees but less than 360 degrees.*
Complementary Angles: *Two angles that add up to 90 degrees.*
Supplementary Angles: *Two angles that up to 180 degrees.*
Vertical Angles: *Angles opposite each other when two lines intersect. They are always equal.*
Adjacent Angles: *Angles that share a common side and vertex but not overlap.*

3.2.1. (Geometry) (Lines & Angles) Parallel Lines and a Transversal

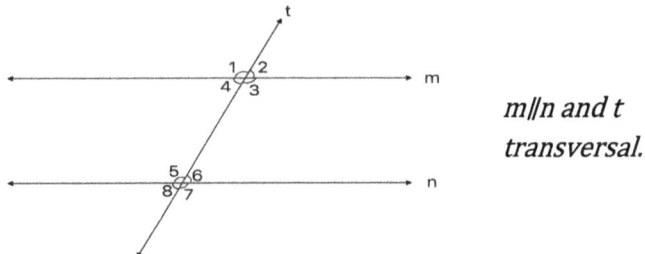

m∥n and t transversal.

Corresponding Angles: *∠1=∠5, ∠2=∠6, ∠3=∠7 and ∠4=∠8*
Alternative Interior Angles: *∠4=∠6 and ∠3=∠5*
Alternative Exterior Angles: *∠1=∠7 and ∠2=∠8*
Interior Angles on the same side of the Transversal or Consecutive Angles or Allied Angles or Co-interior Angles:
∠3+∠6=180° and ∠4+∠5=180°

3.3. (Geometry) Triangles
A triangle is a polygon with three sides and three angles.

3.3.1. (Geometry) (Triangles) Types of Triangles
By Sides:
Equilateral: *All three sides are equal.*
Isosceles: *Two sides are equal.*
Scalene: *All three sides are different.*
By Angles:
Acute: *All three angles are less than 90 degrees.*
Right: *One angle is exactly 90 degrees.*
Obtuse: *One angle is greater than 90 degrees.*

3.3.2. (Geometry) (Triangles) Properties of Triangles
Angle Sum: *The sum of interior angles in a triangle is always 180 degrees.*
Exterior Angle: *An exterior angle of a triangle is equal to the sum of the two non-adjacent interior angles.*
Triangle Inequality Theorem: *The sum of the lengths of any two sides must be greater than the length of the remaining side.*
Congruence: *Two triangles are congruent if their corresponding sides and angles are equal.*
Similarity: *Two triangles are similar if their corresponding angles are equal and their corresponding sides are proportional.*

PROBLEMS IN SCHOOL MATHEMATICS

Property	Congruent Triangle	Similar Triangle
Definition	Triangles that are identical in shape and size	Triangles that have the same shape but may differ in size
Angle Measures	All corresponding angles are equal	All corresponding angles are equal
Side Lengths	All corresponding sides are equal	All corresponding sides are proportional
Area Relationship	Areas are equal if they are congruent	Areas are in proportion to the square of the ratio of corresponding sides
Condition for Formation		
SSS (Side-Side-Side)	All three sides are equal	Corresponding sides are proportional
SAS (Side-Angle-Side)	Two sides are equal, and the included angle is equal	One angle is equal, and the sides including that angle are proportional
ASA (Angle-Side-Angle)	Two angles are equal, and the included side is equal	Two angles are equal (implying similarity)
AAS (Angle-Angle-Side)	Two angles are equal and a non-included side is equal	Two angles are equal (implying similarity)
HL (Hypotenuse-Leg)	Applicable only for right triangles; the hypotenuse and one leg are equal	Not applicable
AA (Angle-Angle)	Not applicable	If two angles are equal, the triangles are similar

PROBLEMS IN SCHOOL MATHEMATICS

Midpoint Theorem of a Triangle & Vice Versa:
I. *In a triangle, the line segment joining the midpoints of two sides is parallel to the third sides and is half the length of the third side.*
II. *If a line is drawn through the midpoint of one side of a triangle, and it is parallel to another side, then it bisects the third side.*

Triangle Centers:

Center	Definition	Location	Special Properties
Centroid (G)	Point of intersection of the medians	Always inside the triangle	Divides each median in a 2:1 ratio.
Circumcenter (O)	Point of intersection of the perpendicular bisectors of the sides	Inside for acute triangles, on the hypotenuse for right triangle, outside for obtuse triangle	Equidistant from all three vertices
Incenter (I)	Point of intersection of the angle bisectors	Always inside the triangle	Equidistant from all the sides
Orthocenter (H)	Point of intersection of altitudes (from a vertex perpendicular to the line containing the opposite side)	Inside for acute triangles, on the vertex of the right angle for right triangles, outside for obtuse triangles	The relationship between sides and angles determines its position

Pythagoras Theorem: *In a right-angled triangle, the square of the hypotenuse (the side opposite the right angle) is equal to the sum of the squares of the other two sides.*
Basic Proportionality Theorem (Thales' Theorem): *If a line segment is drawn parallel to one side of a triangle, it divides the other two sides into segments that are proportional.*
Converse of the Basic Proportionality Theorem: *If a line divides two sides of a triangle proportionally, then it is parallel to the third side.*

3.4. (Geometry) Quadrilateral

A quadrilateral is a polygon with four sides and four angles. The sum of its interior angles is always 360 degrees. In a quadrilateral, diagonals are line segments that connected opposite vertices. Quadrilateral can be classified into several types based on their properties, including:
Square: *All sides are equal, and all angles are 90 degrees.*
Rectangle: *Opposite sides are equal, and all angles are 90 degrees.*
Rhombus: *All sides are equal, but angles are not necessarily 90 degrees.*
Rhomboid: *Opposite sides are equal, and angles are not necessarily 90 degrees.*
Trapezium (or Trapezoid): *At least one pair of opposite sides is parallel.*
Parallelogram: *Opposite sides are equal and parallel, and opposite angles are equal.*

Properties of Diagonals:

I. A diagonal of a parallelogram or rhombus or rectangle or square divides it into two congruent triangles.

II. The diagonals of a parallelogram or rhombus or rectangle or square bisect each other.

III. The diagonals of a rhombus or square are perpendicular to each other.

IV. The diagonals of a rectangle or square are equal in length.

3.5. (Geometry) Circles

A circle is a shape consisting of all points in a plane that is equidistant from a fixed point called the center.

3.5.1. (Geometry) (Circles) Properties of a Circle

Radius: *The distance from the center to any point on the circle. All radii are equal.*

Diameter: *The distance across the circle through the center, equal to twice the radius.*

Circumference: *The distance around the circle, given by $2\pi r$, where r is the radius.*

Area: *The space enclosed by the circle, calculated as πr^2.*

Chord: *A line segment with both end points on the circle. The diameter is the longest chord.*

Arc: *A part of the circumference of the circle.*

Sector: *A region enclosed by two radii and the arc between them.*

Segment: *A region enclosed by a chord and the arc between its endpoints.*
Tangent: *A line that touches the circle at exactly one point.*
Secant: *A secant is a line that intersects a circle at two distinct points.*

3.5.2. (Geometry) (Circles) Fundamental Rules of a Circle

Central Angle: *An angle whose vertex is at the center of the circle. The measure of a central angle is equal to the measure of the arc it intercepts.*

Inscribed Angle: *An inscribed angle in a circle is an angle formed by two chords that share a common endpoint on the circle. The measure of an inscribed angle is half the measure of the central angle that subtends the same arc.*

Angles in a Semicircle: *An angle inscribed in a semicircle is a right angle (90 degrees).*

Angles in the Same Segment: *In a circle, angles in the same segment are angles that subtend the same arc and are formed by drawing two chords from the endpoints of an arc to different points on the circumference. These angles will always be equal.*

Arc Length: *The length of an arc is proportional to its central angle. It can be calculated as* $= \frac{\theta}{360°} \times 2\pi r$ *, where θ is the central angle in degrees and r is the radius.*

Circle Theorem for Chords: *Chords that are equidistance from the center are equal in length. The perpendicular from the center of the circle to a chord bisects the chord.*

Tangent Properties: *A tangent to a circle is perpendicular to the radius at the point of tangency.*

Tangents drawn from an external point to a circle are equal.

Secant-Tangent Theorem: *If a tangent and a secant are drawn from an external point, square of the length of the tangent segment is equal to the product of the lengths of the whole secant segment and its external segment.*

Angle between Chords: *When two chords intersect inside a circle, the measure of the angle formed between the chords is equal to half the sum of the measures of the intercepted arcs.*

Alternate Segment Theorem: *The angle between a tangent and a chord through the point of contact is equal to the angle in the alternate segment of the circle.*

Cyclic Quadrilateral Theorem: *A quadrilateral is cyclic (i.e., all its vertices lie on the circumference of a circle) if and only if the sum of each pair of opposite angles are supplementary.*

3.5.3. (Geometry) (Circles) Types of Circles

- ***Concentric Circles:*** *Circles that share the same center but have different radii.*
- ***Congruent Circles:*** *Circles that have same radius, diameter, and circumference, but do not necessarily share the same center.*
- ***Similar Circles:*** *Circles that have the same shape and proportional measurements, through they can differ in size.*

> ***Tangent Circles:*** *Circles that touch each other at exactly one point. They can be either:*
>   I. ***Internally Tangent:*** *One circles lies inside the other and they touch at one point.*
>   II. ***Externally Tangent:*** *The circles are outside each other and touch at one point.*
> ***Eccentric Circles:*** *Circles that do not share the same center, so they are not concentric. They may intersect or be separate.*
> ***Orthogonal Circles:*** *Circles that intersect each other at right angles (90 degrees).*
> ***Unit Circles:*** *A circle with a radius of 1, commonly used in trigonometry on a coordinate plane.*

3.6. (Geometry) Polygon
A polygon is a two-dimensional geometric figure that is formed by a finite number of straight line segments connected to form a closed shape.

3.6.1. (Geometry) (Polygon) Interior & Exterior Angle
A regular polygon (a polygon where all sides and angles are equal) with n number of sides is given by:

$$Interior\ Angle = \frac{(n-2) \times 180°}{n}$$

$$Exterior\ Angle = \frac{360°}{n}$$

$$Sum\ of\ Interior\ Angles = (n-2) \times 180°$$

$$Sum\ of\ Exterior\ Angles = 360°$$

3.6.2. (Geometry) (Polygon) Number of Diagonals
Number of Diagonals of a Polygon $= \frac{n(n-3)}{2}$, where n is the number of sides in the polygon.

3.7. (Geometry) Non-Euclidean Geometry
Non-Euclidean geometry is a branch of geometry that explores geometries where Euclid's fifth postulate (also known as the parallel postulate) does not hold.
There are two main types of non-Euclidean geometries:
<u>Hyperbolic Geometry:</u> In hyperbolic geometry, through a point not on a given line, there are infinitely many lines that can be drawn parallel to the given line. Hyperbolic geometry has a negative curvature.
<u>Elliptical Geometry (Riemannian Geometry):</u> Elliptic geometry is characterized by the property that there are no parallel lines. All lines eventually intersect. Elliptical geometry has a positive curvature.

PROBLEMS IN SCHOOL MATHEMATICS

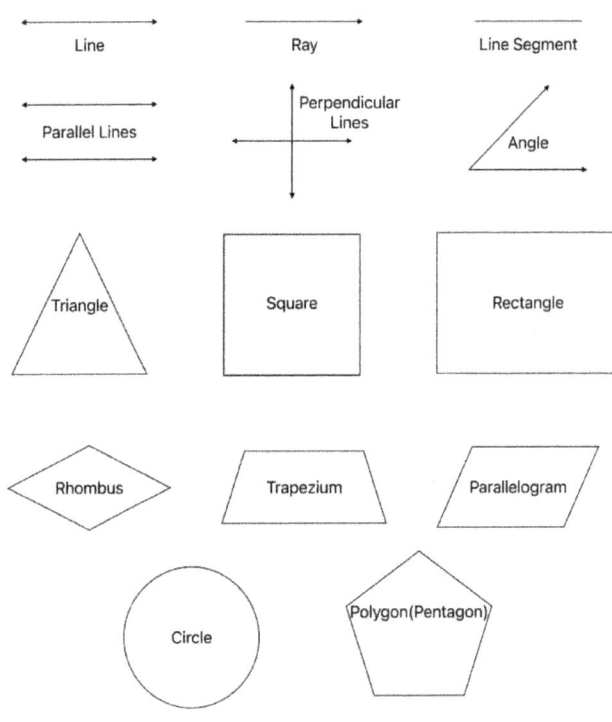

PROBLEMS IN SCHOOL MATHEMATICS

Problems

Geometry (Lines & Angles) 1
∠ABD = ∠ACE, find ∠BAC?

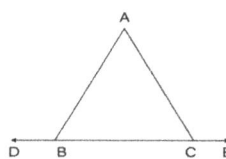

Hint
∠ABD = ∠ACE
Or, 180°− ∠ABC = 180°− ∠ACB
(Linear pair of angles)

Geometry (Lines & Angles) 2
Ray CD and CF bisect the ∠ACE and ∠BCE respectively. Prove that ∠ACD +∠BCF = 90°.

Hint
∠ACE + ∠BCE = 180°
(Linear pair of angles)
Or, $\frac{1}{2}\angle ACE + \frac{1}{2}\angle BCE = \frac{1}{2} \times 180°$

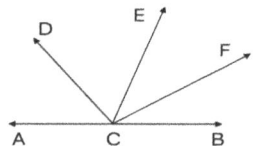

Geometry (Lines & Angles) 3
AB ∥ CD, find the value of x and y?

Hint

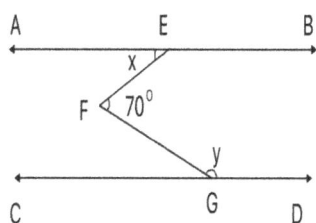

Draw a line parallel to AB and CD

71

Geometry (Lines & Angles) 4

AB || CD

GH and IH are the bisectors of ∠BGI and ∠DIG respectively. If GI = 10 cm and GH = 6 cm, then find IH?

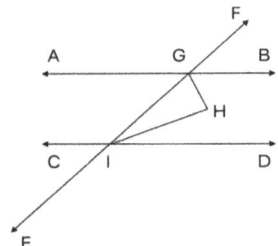

Hint

∠BGI + ∠DIG = 180°
(Co-interior angles)

Or, $\frac{1}{2}$∠BGI + $\frac{1}{2}$∠DIG = $\frac{1}{2} \times 180°$

Geometry (Lines & Angles) 5

AD || EH and CE || AG

If ∠CBD = 70°, then find ∠GFH?

Hint

∠CBD = ∠ABE = 70°
(Vertically opposite angles)

∠BEF = 180° − ∠ABE
(Co-interior angles)

∠AFE = 180° − ∠BEF
(Co-interior angles)

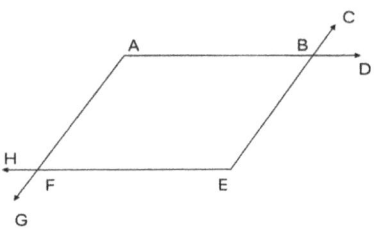

∠GFH = ∠AFE (Vertically Opposite angles)

PROBLEMS IN SCHOOL MATHEMATICS

Geometry (Lines & Angles) 6
AB ∥ CD and EF ∥ GH
If ∠GFH = 30° and ∠GHB = 50°, then find ∠FGH + ∠FEG?

Hint

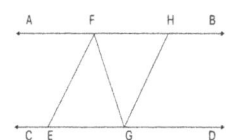

∠GHB = ∠EFH (Co-interior angles)
∠EFG = ∠EFH − ∠GFH
∠FGH = ∠EFG
(Alternate interior angles)
∠AFE = 180° − ∠EFH (Linear pair of angles)
∠FEG = ∠AFE (Alternate interior angles)

Geometry (Lines & Angles) 7
AF ∥ KG, ∠BJK = 60° and ∠DHJ = 110°
Find ∠ABC + ∠BID + ∠FDE?
Hint
∠BJK = ∠JBD
(Alternate interior angles)
∠DHJ + ∠BDH = 180°
(Co-interior angles)

Geometry (Lines & Angles) 8
AB ∥ CD
If ∠GFB = 100° and ∠EGH = 130°, then find x?

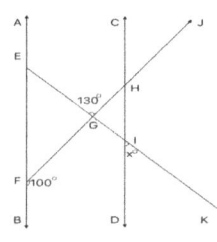

Hint
∠BFG + ∠GHI = 180°
(Co-interior angles)
∠EGH + ∠HGI = 180°
(Linear pair of angles)

73

PROBLEMS IN SCHOOL MATHEMATICS

Geometry (Lines & Angles) 9
$m \parallel n$
Find a, b, c, d, x, y and z?

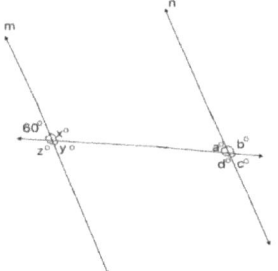

Hint
Alternate interior angles and corresponding angles are equal.

Geometry (Lines & Angles) 10
If $\angle BAC = 50°$ and $\angle ABC = 60°$, then find $\angle ACD$ and $\angle DCE$?

Hint
$\angle ACB =$
$180° - (\angle BAC + \angle ABC)$
$= 7x°$ (Angle sum property of a triangle)

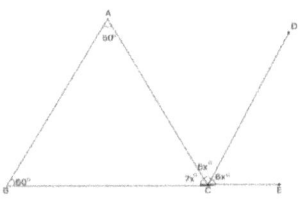

Geometry (Triangles) 11
ABD and BCD are two right angle triangle where AB = CD. Find the angle $\angle ABC$?

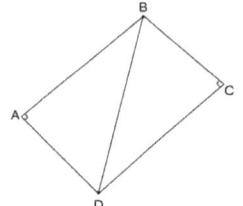

Hint
First prove that, $\triangle ABD \cong \triangle CBD$

PROBLEMS IN SCHOOL MATHEMATICS

Geometry (Triangles) 12
AC is the bisector of ∠A and ∠B = ∠D = 90°. If AB = 7 cm and CD = 4 cm, then find the value BC and AD?

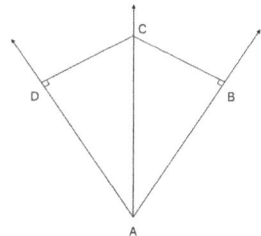

Hint
First prove that, △ABC ≅ △ADC

Geometry (Triangles) 13
ABC and ADC are two isosceles triangle, where AB = BC and AD = DC, show that △ABD ≅ △CBD.

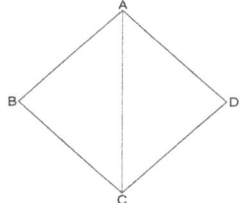

Hint
Join BD, and then prove that △ABD ≅ △CBD

Geometry (Triangles) 14
∠C = ∠B and ∠AEB = ∠ADC
If AB = AC and CD = 10 cm, then find the value of BE?

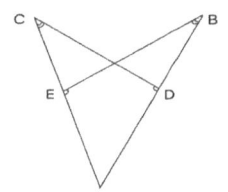

Hint
First prove that △ACD ≅ △ABE

PROBLEMS IN SCHOOL MATHEMATICS

Geometry (Triangles) 15
AD is the bisector of ∠BAC and AB = AC, then prove that AD is the perpendicular bisector of BC.

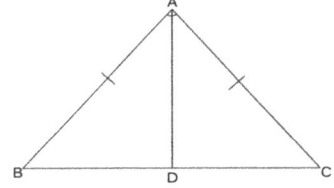

Hint
First prove that
△ ABD ≅ △ACD

Geometry (Triangles) 16
CE ⊥ AB and BD ⊥ AC, find the relation between ∠ABD and ∠ACE?

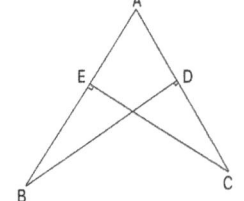

Hint
First prove that △ABD ≅ △ACE

Geometry (Triangles) 17
If EF ∥ BD ∥ GH, then show that $\frac{AD}{CD}=\frac{AE}{CG}$ and $\frac{AB}{CB}=\frac{AF}{CH}$.

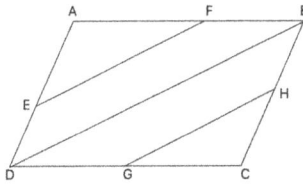

Hint
Apply proportionality theorem on △ABD and △CBD

Geometry (Triangles) 18

$BA \perp AD$,
$\angle ACB = 60°$ and $\angle ADB = 30°$, find the value of x?

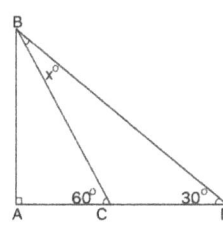

Hint
$\angle ABC =$
$180° - (\angle BAC + \angle ACB)$
And $\angle ABD =$
$180° - (\angle BAC + \angle ADB)$
$\therefore x = \angle CBD = \angle ABD - \angle ABC$

Geometry (Triangles) 19

$\angle ABC = 70°$ and $\angle ACB = 50°$, BD and CD bisects $\angle B$ and $\angle C$ respectively. Find the value of $\angle BDC$?

Hint
$\angle BDC =$
$180° - \frac{1}{2}(\angle ABC + \angle ACB)$

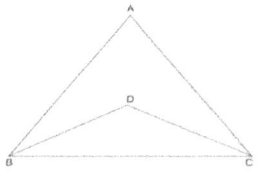

Geometry (Triangles) 20

If $\angle EBC = 40°$ and $\angle BCD = 30°$, $CD \perp AB$ and $BE \perp AC$, then find $\angle BAC$, $\angle ABC$ and $\angle ACB$?

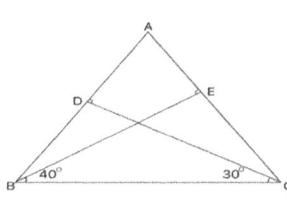

Hint
$\angle ACB =$
$180° - (\angle EBC + \angle BEC)$
$\angle ABC =$
$180° - (\angle CDB + \angle BCD)$

Geometry (Quadrilaterals) 21

In $\triangle ABC$, $\angle A : \angle B : \angle C = 5:6:7$, find the shortest and longest side of triangle?

Hint

Largest angle opposite side longest and Smallest angle opposite side shortest

Geometry (Quadrilaterals) 22

ABCD is a rhombus, then show that $\triangle CDE \cong \triangle CBE$ and $\triangle ADE \cong \triangle ABE$.

Hint

First prove that,
$\triangle ABC \cong \triangle ADC$

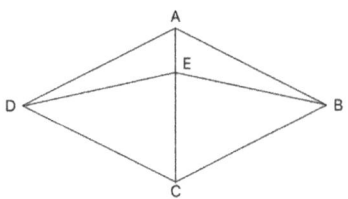

Geometry (Quadrilaterals) 23

ABCD is a trapezium in which AB ∥ DC. If BC = 12 cm and $\angle C = 45°$, then find the distance between AB and CD?

Hint

Draw a perpendicular from point B on side CD

PROBLEMS IN SCHOOL MATHEMATICS

Geometry (Quadrilaterals) 24
ABCD is a rectangle, where AB = 8 cm and BC = 6 cm. Find the value of OC?

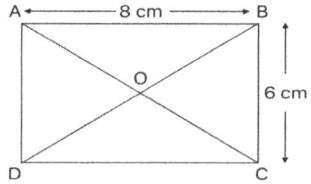

Hint
Diagonals of rectangle are equal and bisect each other.

Geometry (Quadrilaterals) 25
In ABCD quadrilateral ∠B = 30° and ∠C = 120°. AE and DE is the bisector of ∠A and ∠D respectively. Find ∠AED?

Hint
∠A + ∠B + ∠C + ∠D = 360°
And ∠AED =
$180° - \frac{1}{2}(\angle A + \angle D)$

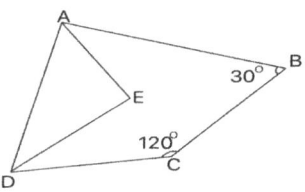

Geometry (Quadrilaterals) 26
ABCD is a parallelogram, where ∠CBE = 100° and ∠ABD = 30°. Find the value of x and y?

Hint
∠BAD = x° = ∠CBE = 100° (Opposite sides of parallelogram are parallel, so these are corresponding angles)

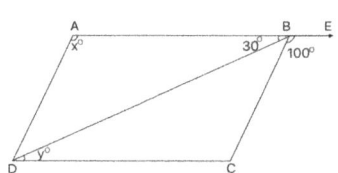

∠BAD = ∠BCD (Opposite angles of parallelogram are equal)

79

Geometry (Quadrilaterals) 27

ABCD is a parallelogram. Find the value of x?

Hint

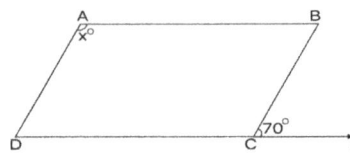

Opposite angles of parallelogram are equal.
∠BAD = x° = ∠BCD = 180° − ∠BCE

Geometry (Quadrilaterals) 28

ABCD is a parallelogram. Find the value of x and y?

Hint

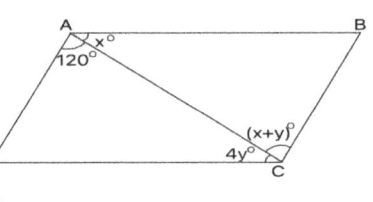

Opposite sides of parallelogram are parallel.
∴ ∠CAD = ∠ACB and ∠BAC = ∠ACD
(Alternate interior angles)

Geometry (Circles) 29

ABC is a secant and AD is a tangent to the circle from point A. If AD = 7 cm and AB = 5 cm, then find the value of BC.

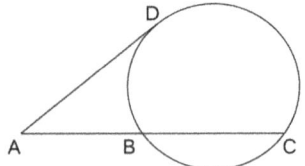

Hint

$AB \times AC = AD^2$

Geometry (Circles) 30

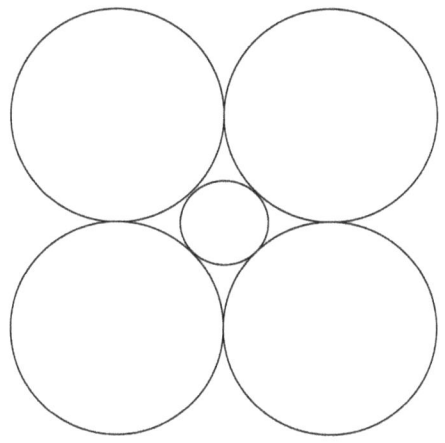

Find the relation between big and small circles diameters?
Hint

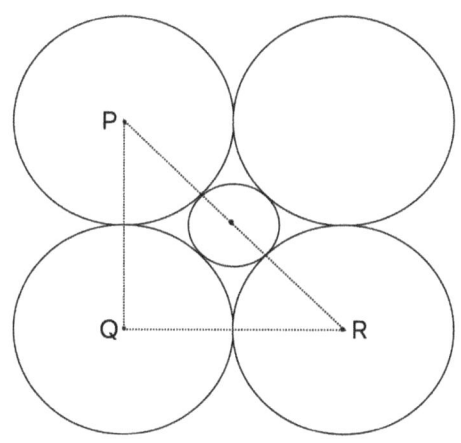

PR = Diameter of big circle + Diameter of small circle
PQ = Diameter of big circle
And $\angle Q = 90°$

Geometry (Circles) 31

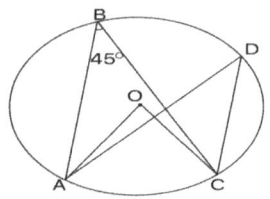

'O' is the centre of the circle. If ∠ABC = 45°, then find ∠AOC and ∠ADC?

Hint

∠ABC = ∠ADC (Angles in the same segment of a circle are equal)

And ∠AOC = 2∠ABC (Angles in the same segment at the centre is double by any point on the remaining part of the circle)

Geometry (Circles) 32

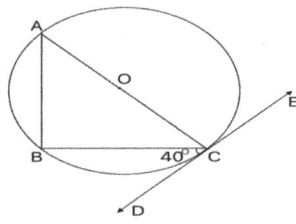

'O' is the centre of the circle. If ∠BCD = 40°, then find ∠BAC?

Hint

∠ABC = 90° (Angle of semicircle)

And ∠ACD = 90° (Tangent is perpendicular to the circle)

∴ ∠BAC = 180°−[∠ABC + (∠ACD − ∠BCD)] (Angle sum property of a triangle)

Geometry (Circles) 33

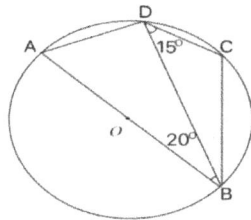

'O' is the centre of the circle.
If ∠BDC = 15° and ∠ABD = 20°, then find ∠BCD?
Hint
∠BDA = 90° (Angle of semicircle)
∠ABC = 180° − ∠ADC (Sum of opposite angles of a cyclic quadrilateral is 180°)
Or, ∠ABD + ∠CBD = 180° − (∠BDC + ∠BDA)
Therefore, ∠BCD = 180° − (∠BDC + ∠CBD) (Angle sum property of a triangle)

Geometry (Circles) 34

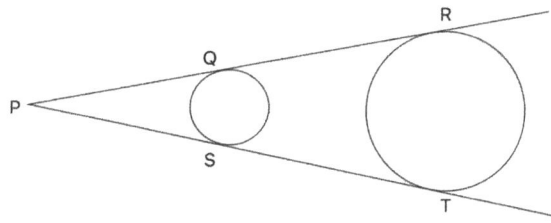

If QR = 10 cm and PT = 15 cm, find PQ and ST?
Hint
PR = PT and PQ = PS (The lengths of tangents drawn from an external point to a circle are equal)

Geometry (Circles) 35

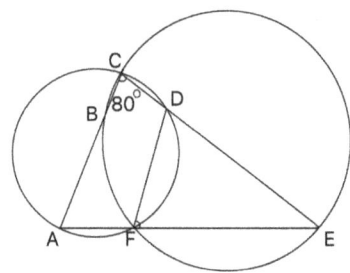

If ∠ACE = 80°, then find ∠DFE?
Hint
∠AFD = 180° − ∠ACE (ACDF is a cyclic quadrilateral)

Geometry (Circles) 36

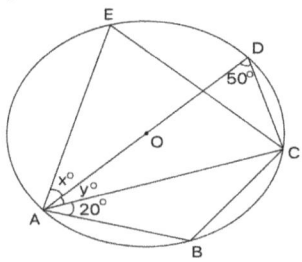

'O' is the centre of the circle. Find the value of x and y?
Hint
ABCD is a cyclic quadrilateral.
∠ADC + ∠BAD + ∠BCD + ∠ABC = 360°
Or, ∠ADC + ∠BAD + (180° − ∠BAD) + (180° − ∠ADC) = 360°
ABCE is a cyclic quadrilateral.
∠ACD = 90° (Angle on semicircle)
∠AEC = ∠ADC = 50° (Angles in the same segment of a circle are equal)

PROBLEMS IN SCHOOL MATHEMATICS

Geometry (Circles) 37

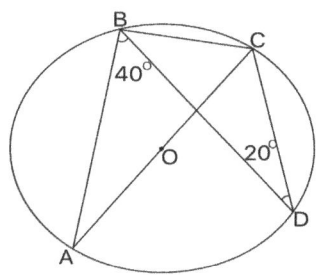

'O' is the centre of the circle.
If $\angle BDC = 20°$ and $\angle ABD = 40°$, then find $\angle CBD$?

Hint

$\angle ABC = 90°$ (Angle on semicircle)
$\angle BAC = \angle BDC = 20°$ & $\angle ABD = \angle ACD = 40°$
(Angles on the same segment of a circle are equal)
$\angle ACB = 180° - (\angle ABC + \angle BAC)$
(Angle sum property of triangle)

Geometry (Circles) 38

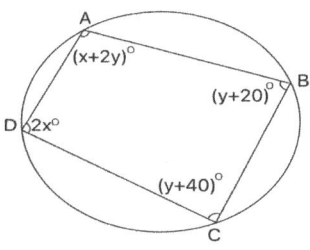

ABCD is a cyclic quadrilateral. Find the value of x and y?

Hint

$\angle A + \angle C = 180°$ & $\angle B + \angle D = 180°$
(ABCD is a cyclic quadrilateral)

Geometry (Circles) 39

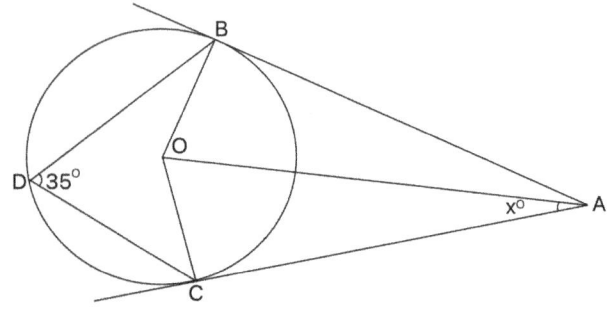

AB and AC are tangents to the circle, with centre 'O'.
If ∠BDC = 35°, then find the value of x?
Hint
∠BOC = 2∠BDC (Angles in the same segment at the centre is double by any point on the remaining part of the circle)
∠BAO = ∠CAO, because △AOB ≅ △AOC

Geometry (Circles) 40

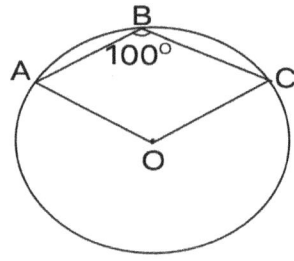

'O' is the centre of the circle.
If ∠ABC = 100°, then find the value of ∠AOC?
Hint
Take a point D on arc AC.

MENSURATION

4. Mensuration
Mensuration is the branch of mathematics that deals with the measurement of geometric figures and shapes, including their area, volume and surface area.

4.1. (Mensuration) Triangle
$Area = \frac{1}{2} \times a \times b \times \sin\theta$,

Where a and b are the lengths of two sides and θ is the included angle between those sides.

$Area(using\ Heron's\ Formula) = \sqrt{s(s-a)(s-b)(s-c)}$

Where a, b, c are the lengths of the sides and

$semi-perimeter(s) = \frac{a+b+c}{2}$.

Radius of Centroid, Incenter, Orthocenter, Circumcenter:

$Centroid\ Radius$
$= \frac{2}{3} \times \frac{Side\ Length \times Side\ Lenght \times Side\ Lenght}{4 \times Area\ of\ the\ Triangle}$

$Inradius$
$= \frac{Area\ of\ the\ Triangle}{Semi-Perimeter\ of\ the\ Triangle}$

$Orthoradius = Circumradius$
$= \frac{Side\ Length \times Side\ Lenght \times Side\ Lenght}{4 \times Area\ of\ the\ Triangle}$

4.2. (Mensuration) Quadrilateral

$$Area = \frac{1}{2} \times d_1 \times d_2 \times \sin\theta$$

The lengths of the diagonals d_1 and d_2 and the angle θ between them.

For a Cyclic Quadrilateral (Using Brahmagupta's Formula)

$$Area = \sqrt{s(s-a)(s-b)(s-c)(s-d)}$$

Where a, b, c and d are the length of all four sides and $semi-perimeter(s) = \frac{a+b+c+d}{2}$.

- Area of Square
  $= (Lenght\ of\ the\ Side)_1 \times (Lenght\ of\ the\ Side)_2$
- Area of Reactangle $= Lenght \times Width$
- Area of Rhombus
  $= \frac{1}{2} \times (Lenght\ of\ the\ Diagonal)_1$
  $\times (Lenght\ of\ the\ Diagonal)_2$
- Area of Parallelogram $= Base \times Height$
- Area of Trapezium
  $= \frac{1}{2} \times (Sum\ of\ Lenghts\ of\ two\ Parallel\ Sides) \times Height$

4.3. (Mensuration) Shoelace Formula (Gauss's Area Formula)

$$Area = \frac{1}{2}\left|\sum_{i=1}^{n-1}(x_i \cdot y_{i+1} - y_i \cdot x_{i+1}) + (x_n \cdot y_1 - y_n \cdot x_1)\right|,$$

Where $(x_1, y_1), (x_2, y_2), \ldots\ldots\ldots (x_n, y_n)$ are the coordinates of the vertices of a polygon.

4.4. (Mensuration) Circle

$Area = \pi \times r^2$, where r is the radius of the circle.

PROBLEMS IN SCHOOL MATHEMATICS

4.4.1. (Mensuration) (Circle) Area of a Sector of a Circle
$Area\ of\ Sector = \frac{\theta}{360°} \times \pi r^2$, *where θ is the central angle in degrees and r is the radius.*

4.4.2. (Mensuration) (Circle) Area of a Segment of a Circle
$Area\ of\ Segment = Area\ of\ Sector - Area\ of\ Triangle$
$= Area\ of\ Sector - \frac{1}{2} \times r^2 \times \sin\theta$, *where r is the radius of the circle and θ is the central angle in radians.*

4.4.3. (Mensuration) (Circle) Area of an Annulus (Area between two Concentric Circle)
$Area\ of\ Annulus = \pi(R^2 - r^2)$, *where R is the radius of outer circle and r is the radius of inner circle.*

4.5. (Mensuration) Cube
A cube is a three dimensional geometric shape with six equal faces, twelve equal edges, and eight vertices. Each face of a cube is a square; all angles between the faces are right angles. In a cube, all edges have same length.
$Surface\ Area = 6 \times a^2$
$Volume = a^3$, *where a is the length of one side of the cube.*

4.6. (Mensuration) Cuboid
A cuboid is a three dimensional geometric shape with six rectangular faces, twelve edges, and eight vertices. All its angles are right angles, and opposite faces are congruent.
$Surface\ Area = 2(lw + lh + wh)$

$Volume = l \times w \times h$, where l = length, w = width, h = height.

4.7. (Mensuration) Cylinder
A cylinder is a three-dimensional shape with two parallel circular bases connected by a curved surface. The height is the perpendicular distance between the bases.
$Surface\ Area = 2\pi r(r + h)$
$Volume = \pi r^2 h$, where is r the radius of the base and h is the height.

4.8. (Mensuration) Cone
A cone is a three-dimensional shape with a circular base and a single curved surface that tapers to a point called the apex.
$Volume = \frac{1}{3}\pi r^2 h$, where r is the radius of the base and h is the height.
$Surface\ Area = \pi r(r + l)$, where l is the slant height, calculate as $\sqrt{r^2 + h^2}$.

4.9. (Mensuration) Frustum
A frustum is geometric shape that results from slicing a cone or pyramid with a plane parallel to its base. It has two parallel, congruent bases and lateral faces that are typically trapezoidal.
$Surface\ Area = \pi(r_1^2 + r_2^2) + \pi(r_1 + r_2)l$

$Volume = \frac{1}{3}\pi h(r_1^2 + r_1 r_2 + r_2^2)$, where r_1 and r_2 are the radii of the top and bottom bases, h is the height and l is the slant height.

4.10. (Mensuration) Prism
A prism is a three dimensional geometric shape with two parallel, congruent bases connected by a rectangular or parallelogram faces.
Surface Area = 2 × Base area + Lateral Area
Volume = Base Area × h , where h is the height.

4.11. (Mensuration) Pyramid
A pyramid is a three dimensional geometric shape with a polygonal base and triangular faces that meet at a single point called the apex.
Surface Area = Base Area + Lateral Area
$Volume = \frac{1}{3} \times Base\ Area \times h$, where h is the height.

4.12. (Mensuration) Sphere
A sphere is a perfectly symmetrical three-dimensional shape where every point on its surface is equidistant from its center.
$Surface\ Area = 4\pi r^2$
$Volume = \frac{4}{3}\pi r^3$, where r is the radius of the sphere.

4.13. (Mensuration) Hemisphere
A hemisphere is half of a sphere, divided by a plane that passes through its center. It has a curved surface that is half of the sphere's surface area and a flat circular base.
$Surface\ Area = 3\pi r^2$
$Volume = \frac{2}{3}\pi r^3$, where r is the radius of the hemisphere.

4.14. (Mensuration) Torus
A torus is a three dimensional shape resembling a doughnut or a ring. It is formed by rotating a circle in three-dimensional space around an axis that lies in the same plane as the circle but does not intersect it.
$Surface\ Area = 4\pi^2 Rr$
$Volume = 2\pi^2 Rr^2$, where R is the major radius and r is the minor radius.

Problems

Mensuration (Triangles) 1
The lengths of two adjacent sides of triangle are 10 cm and 15 cm. If the angle between the sides is 30°, find the area of the triangle?

Hint

Area of triangle $= \frac{1}{2} \times 10 \times 15 \times \sin 30°$ cm^2.

Mensuration (Triangles) 2
Ankita is planning to fertilize her flower garden. Each bag of fertilizer claims to cover 100 m^2 of area. Her property of land is approximately in the shape of triangle. She measures sides of her yard to be 60 m, 70 m and 80 m. How many bags of fertilizer must she buy?

Hint

Number of bags $= \dfrac{\text{Area of triangle using Heron's formula}}{100 \; m^2}$.

Mensuration (Cuboids) 3
Ananya's hall is 15 m long and 10 m broad. If the sum of the areas of the floor and the ceiling is equal to the sum of the areas of four walls, find the volume of the hall?

Hint

$2(l + b) \times h = 2lb$, where $l = 15$ m and $b = 10$ m.

Mensuration (Cuboids) 4

Karnajit's 100 cows are taking a dip into a cuboidal lake

which is 1000 m long and 100 m broad. What is the rise of water level in the lake, if the average displacement of the water by a cow is 0.10 m³?

Hint

Volume of rise of water level in the lake =
Average displacement of water by 100 cows
Therefore, $1000 \times 100 \times height = 100 \times 0.10$

Mensuration (Cuboids) 5

In a shower, 10 cm of rain falls. Find the volume of water falls on 2 hectares of ground?

Hint

Area = 2 hectares = $(2 \times 10000) m^2$
Depth = $\frac{10}{100}$ m
Volume = Area × Depth $Unit^3$

PROBLEMS IN SCHOOL MATHEMATICS

Mensuration (Cuboids & Cubes) 6
Ten equal cubes of side 10 cm are joined end to end. Find the surface area of the resulting cuboid?
Hint
Length of cuboid $= 10 \times 10 = 100$ cm
Breadth of cuboid $= 10$ cm
Height of cuboid $= 10$ cm

Mensuration (Cylinders) 7
Barish's paint roller is cylinder in shape. It has a diameter of 10 cm and a width of 35 cm. Find the area painted by the roller when it makes 100 revolutions, correct to the nearest 0.1 cm².
Hint
Area painted by the roller of 100 revolutions
$= 100 \times$ Curved surface area of cylinder shape roller.

Mensuration (Cylinders) 8
The respective ratio of radii of two right circular cylinders is 2:3. The respective ratio of volumes of cylinders is 9:7, and then what is the ratio of heights cylinders?
Hint
$$\frac{Volume\ of\ first\ cylinder}{Volume\ of\ second\ cylinder} = \frac{\pi r_1^2 h_1}{\pi r_2^2 h_2} = \frac{9}{7}$$

PROBLEMS IN SCHOOL MATHEMATICS

Mensuration (Cylinders) 9

Parthib's hollow iron pipe is 17 cm long and its external diameter is 6 cm. If the thickness of the pipe is 2 cm and iron weighs 10 g/cm³, then find the weight of the pipe?

Hint

External radius $= \frac{6}{2} = 3\ cm$
Internal radius $= (3 - 2) = 1\ cm$
Therefore,
weight of iron
$= \pi \times [(3)^2 - (1)^2] \times 17 \times 10\ gm$

Mensuration (Cylinders) 10

Jayeeta's well of inner diameter 12 m is dug to depth of 24 m. Earth taken out of it has been evenly spread around it to a width of 6 cm to form an embarkment. Find the height of the embarkment so formed?

Hint

Volume of Earth taken out = Volume of embarkment

Mensuration (Cylinders & Cuboids) 11

What part of a ditch 60 m long, 24 m broad and 8 m deep can be filled by the earth got digging a cylindrical tunnel of diameter 8 m and length 64 m?

Hint

Part required $= \frac{Volume\ of\ cylindrical\ tunnel}{Volume\ of\ ditch}$

PROBLEMS IN SCHOOL MATHEMATICS

Mensuration (Cones) 12
If the radius of right circular cone is increased by r% without increasing the height, then what is the percentage increase in the volume of the cone?

Hint

Percentage increase in the volume $= \dfrac{\frac{1}{3}\pi r_2^2 h - \frac{1}{3}\pi r_1^2 h}{\frac{1}{3}\pi r_1^2 h} \times 100$

Where $r_2 = \left(\dfrac{100+r}{100}\right) r_1$

Mensuration (Cylinders & Cones) 13
Swagata's ice-cream, completely filled in a cylinder of diameter 49 cm and height 40 cm, is to be served by completely filling Payel's identical disposable cones of diameter 4 cm and height 7 cm. Find the maximum number of persons that can be served in this way?

Hint

Numbers of persons $= \dfrac{Volume\ of\ the\ cylinder}{Volume\ of\ the\ cone}$

Mensuration (Cylinders & Cones) 14
Barnik's solid consists of circular cylinder with exact fitting right circular cone placed on top. The height of the cone is h. If the total volume of the solid is nine times the volume of cone, then find the height of the circular cylinder?

Hint

Volume of solid $= 9 \times$ Volume of circular cone
∴ (Volume of cylinder + Volume of cone)
$= 9 \times$ Volume of cone

Mensuration (Frustums) 15

Sayanika's drinking water glass of height 30 cm is in the shape of frustum of a cone and diameters of its bottom and top circular ends are 8 cm and 12 cm respectively. Find the capacity of the glass?

Hint

$h = 30$ cm, $R = \frac{12}{2}$ cm, $r = \frac{8}{2}$ cm

$\therefore$ Capacity of glass $= \frac{\pi h}{3}(r^2 + R^2 + rR)$ Unit³

Mensuration (Spheres) 16

If the radius of the sphere is decreased by p%, by what percent does its surface area decrease?

Hint

Percentage decrease in surface area

$= \frac{4\pi r_2^2 - 4\pi r_1^2}{4\pi r_1^2} \times 100$

Where $r_2 = \left(\frac{100 - p}{100}\right) r_1$

Mensuration (Spheres) 17

The diameter of Sun is approximately 110 times of the diameter of the Earth. What fraction of the volume of the Sun is the volume of the Earth?

PROBLEMS IN SCHOOL MATHEMATICS

Hint

$$\frac{Volume\ of\ Earth}{Volume\ of\ Sun} = \frac{\frac{4}{3}\pi\left(\frac{Diameter\ of\ Earth}{2}\right)^3}{\frac{4}{3}\pi\left(\frac{110 \times Diameter\ of\ Earth}{2}\right)^3}$$

Mensuration (Spheres) 18
The radius of sphere is 8 cm. It is melted and drawn into a wire of radius 0.4 cm. Find the length of the wire?

Hint
Volume of wire (Wire in cylindrical shape)
= Volume of Sphere

Mensuration (Spheres & Cubes) 19
What is the volume of the largest sphere that can be curved out of a cube of edge 9 cm?

Hint
Diameter of sphere = Side of cube

Mensuration (Spheres & Hemispheres) 20
Baidhayan's sphere and hemisphere have the same surface area. Find the ratio of their volumes?

Hint
Surface area of sphere = Surface area of hemisphere
∴ $4\pi r_1^2 = 3\pi r_2^2$,
where r_1 = Sphere radius & r_2 = Hemisphere radius.

PROBLEMS IN SCHOOL MATHEMATICS

SEQUENCE & SERIES

5. Sequence & Series
A sequence is an ordered list of numbers or terms, where each term is defined by a specific rule or pattern.
A series, on the other hand, is the sum of the terms of a sequence.

5.1. (Sequence & Series) Arithmetic Progression
An arithmetic progression (AP) is a sequence of numbers in which the difference between consecutive terms is constant.
nth term, $a_n = a_1 + (n-1)d$, where a_1 is the first term, d is the common difference.
The sum of the first n terms, $S_n = \frac{n}{2}[2a_1 + (n-1)d]$ or equivalently $S_n = \frac{n}{2}(a_1 + a_n)$
The arithmetic mean (AM) of numbers a and b in an arithmetic progression is given by:
$$AM = \frac{a+b}{2}$$

5.2. (Sequence & Series) Geometric Progression
A geometric progression (GP) is a sequence where each term after the first is found by multiplying the previous term by a constant factor, called the common ratio r.
nth term, $a_n = a_1 r^{(n-1)}$, where a_1 is the first term and r is the common ratio.

The sum of the first n terms, $S_n = a_1 \frac{1-r^n}{1-r}$ for $r \neq 1$

If $r = 1$, the sum is simply $S_n = n.a_1$.

The geometric mean (GM) of numbers a and b in a geometric progression is given by:

$GM = \sqrt{ab}$

5.3. (Sequence & Series) Harmonic Progression

A harmonic progression (HP) is a sequence of numbers where the reciprocals of the terms from an arithmetic progression (AP)

If a_1, a_2 and a_3 is a harmonic progression, then $\frac{1}{a_1}, \frac{1}{a_2}$ and $\frac{1}{a_3}$ forms an arithmetic progression.

The harmonic mean (HM) of numbers a and b in a harmonic progression is given by:

$$HM = \frac{2ab}{a+b}$$

5.4. (Sequence & Series) Properties of Sigma Notation

- $\sum_{i=m}^{n}(a_i + b_i) = \sum_{i=m}^{n} a_i + \sum_{i=m}^{n} b_i$
- $\sum_{i=m}^{n} c.a_i = c\sum_{i=m}^{n} a_i$, where c is a constant.
- $\sum_{i=m}^{n} a_i = \sum_{j=m}^{n} a_j$, where $j = i$
- $\sum_{i=m}^{n} a_i = -\sum_{i=n}^{m} a_i$
- $\sum_{i=m}^{n} a_i = \sum_{i=m}^{k} a_i + \sum_{i=k+1}^{n} a_i$, for $m \leq k < n$
- $\sum_{i=1}^{n} c = n.c$, where c is a constant.
- $\sum_{i=0}^{n} ar^i = a\frac{1-r^{n+1}}{1-r}$, for $r \neq 1$
- $\sum_{i=1}^{n} i = \frac{n(n+1)}{2}$

- $\sum_{i=1}^{n} i^2 = \frac{n(n+1)(2n+1)}{6}$
- $\sum_{i=1}^{n} i^3 = \left(\frac{n(n+1)}{n}\right)^2$
- $\sum_{i=1}^{n} a_i + \sum_{i=1}^{n} b_i = \sum_{i=1}^{n}(a_i + b_i)$

5.5. (Sequence & Series) Famous Infinite Series

p-Series:

$$S = \sum_{n=1}^{\infty} \frac{1}{n^p}$$

Where p is a constant

Telescoping Series:

$$S = \sum_{n=1}^{N} \left(\frac{1}{n} - \frac{1}{n+1}\right)$$

Euler's Series for π:

$$\sum_{n=1}^{\infty} \frac{1}{n^2} = \frac{\pi^2}{6}$$

Exponential Series:

$$e^x = \sum_{n=0}^{\infty} \frac{x^n}{n!}$$

Sine and Cosine Series:

$$\sin(x) = \sum_{n=0}^{\infty} \frac{(-1)^n x^{2n+1}}{(2n+1)!}$$

$$\cos(x) = \sum_{n=0}^{\infty} \frac{(-1)^n x^{2n}}{(2n)!}$$

PROBLEMS IN SCHOOL MATHEMATICS

Natural Logarithm Series:
$$\ln(1+x) = \sum_{n=1}^{\infty} \frac{(-1)^{n+1} x^n}{n}, for\ |x| < 1$$

Binomial Series:
$$(1+x)^\alpha = \sum_{n=0}^{\infty} \binom{\alpha}{n} x^n = 1 + \alpha x + \frac{\alpha(\alpha-1)}{2!} x^2 + \ldots\ldots$$

For any real number α

Riemann Zeta Function Series:
$$\zeta(p) = \sum_{n=1}^{\infty} \frac{1}{n^p}$$

Where p *is a constant*

PROBLEMS IN SCHOOL MATHEMATICS

Problems

Sequence & Series (Arithmetic Progression) 1
Find the pth term of an AP, sum of whose first n terms is $(n + 1) + 2(n + 1)^2$.
Hint
p^{th} term = Sum of p terms – Sum of (p–1) terms
$= [(p + 1) + 2(p + 1)^2] - [(p - 1 + 1) + 2(p - 1 + 1)^2]$

Sequence & Series (Arithmetic Progression) 2
Find the sum of n terms of the AP, whose r^{th} term is $\frac{(r + 1)^3}{r + 2}$.
Hint
Common difference (d) = Second term – First term
$= \frac{(2 + 1)^3}{2 + 2} - \frac{(1 + 1)^3}{1 + 2}$

Sequence & Series (Arithmetic Progression) 3
If the sum of first m terms of an AP is two times to the sum of first n terms, then find the sum of first $(m + n)$ terms.
Hint
Sum of first m terms = 2 × Sum of first n terms
$S_m = 2S_n$

Sequence & Series (Arithmetic Progression) 4
Find the sum of n terms of
$a \times b + (a + 2)(b - 3) + (a + 4)(b - 6) + \ldots\ldots\ldots$

PROBLEMS IN SCHOOL MATHEMATICS

Hint
$\{Sum\ of\ n\ terms\ of\ a, (a+2), (a+4) \ldots \ldots\}$
$\qquad \times \{Sum\ of\ n\ terms\ of\ b, (b-3), (b-6) \ldots \ldots\}$

Sequence & Series (Geometric Progression) 5
Insert three terms between 1 to 10000, so that resulting sequence is in GP.
Hint
1st term is 1 and 5th term is 10000

Sequence & Series (Geometric Progression) 6
Find the pth term of $x^2, 1, \frac{1}{x^2} \ldots \ldots \ldots$
Hint
First term $= x^2$
And common ratio $= \frac{1}{x^2}$

Sequence & Series (Geometric Progression) 7
Find the sum up to n terms of the series
$0.m + 0.mm + 0.mmm + 0.mmmm + \ldots\ldots$
Hint
$0.m + 0.mm + 0.mmm + 0.mmmm + \ldots\ldots$ *up to n terms*
$= \frac{m}{9} [0.9 + 0.99 + 0.999 + 0.9999 + \ldots\ldots$ *up to n terms]*.

Sequence & Series (Geometric Progression) 8
If the mth and n^{th} terms of a GP is n and m respectively, then find its $\left(\frac{m+n}{2}\right)^{th}$ term?

Hint

$\dfrac{m^{th}\ term}{n^{th}\ term} = \dfrac{n}{m}$

Or, $\dfrac{ar^{m-1}}{ar^{n-1}} = \dfrac{n}{m}$

Or, $r = \left(\dfrac{n}{m}\right)^{\frac{1}{m-n}}$

Sequence & Series (Geometric Progression) 9
If p, q, r and s are in GP, then find the value of
$$\dfrac{(p^2 + q^2 + r^2)(q^2 + r^2 + s^2)(r^2 + s^2 + p^2)(s^2 + p^2 + q^2)}{pqr + qrs + rsp}$$
; Where first term = common ratio = 1.

Hint

$\dfrac{q}{p} = \dfrac{r}{q} = \dfrac{s}{r} = common\ ratio$

Sequence & Series (Geometric Progression) 10
If two numbers are in the ratio of
$(50 + 7\sqrt{51}) : (50 - 7\sqrt{51})$, *then show that sum of two numbers is 100 times their geometric mean.*

Hint

Use componendo and dividendo.

COORDINATE GEOMETRY

6. Coordinate Geometry

Coordinate geometry, also known as analytic geometry, is the study of geometric figures using a coordinate system. It involves using algebraic methods to analyze and solve geometric problems. In this field, points, lines, and shapes are defined and manipulated using coordinates in a plane (typically Cartesian coordinate with x and y axes) or in space (with x, y and z axes).

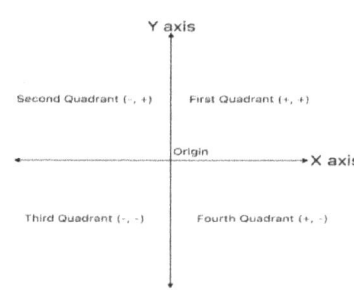

6.1. (Coordinate Geometry) Properties of the Four Quadrants

Aspect	First Quadrant	Second Quadrant	Third Quadrant	Fourth Quadrant
x-coordinate (horizontal)	Positive	Negative	Negative	Positive
y-coordinate (vertical)	Positive	Positive	Negative	Negative
Coordinate Signs	(+,+)	(−,+)	(−,−)	(+,−)
Angle Range	0° to 90°	90° to 180°	180° to 270°	270° to 360°
Vector Direction	North-East	North-West	South-West	South-East

PROBLEMS IN SCHOOL MATHEMATICS

6.2. Equations for the x-axis, y-axis and the Origin
Equation of the x-axis: $y = 0$
Equation of the y-axis: $x = 0$
Equation of the Origin: $x = 0, y = 0$
Equation of a Line Passing through the Origin: $y = mx$, where m is the slope of the line.

6.3. (Coordinate Geometry) Distance Formula
To find the distance d between two points (x_1, y_1) and (x_2, y_2),
$$d = \sqrt{(x_2 - x_1)^2 + (y_2 - y_1)^2}$$

6.4. (Coordinate Geometry) Section Formula
Internal Division: *If a point $P(x, y)$ divides the line segment joining $A(x_1, y_1)$ and $B(x_2, y_2)$ in the ratio $m:n$, then the coordinates of P given by:*
$$x = \frac{mx_2 + nx_1}{m + n}, y = \frac{my_2 + ny_1}{m + n}$$
External Division: *If a point $P(x, y)$ divides the line segment joining $A(x_1, y_1)$ and $B(x_2, y_2)$ in the ratio $m:n$, then the coordinates of P given by:*
$$x = \frac{mx_2 - nx_1}{m - n}, y = \frac{my_2 - ny_1}{m - n}.$$

6.5. (Coordinate Geometry) Area of Triangle
To find the area of a triangle given its vertices are $(x_1, y_1), (x_2, y_2)$ and (x_3, y_3) in the coordinate geometry.
$$\text{Area} = \frac{1}{2} |x_1(y_2 - y_3) + x_2(y_3 - y_1) + x_3(y_1 - y_2)|.$$

6.6. (Coordinate Geometry) Slope Formula
The slope m of a line passing through (x_1, y_1) and (x_2, y_2) is $= \frac{y_2 - y_1}{x_2 - x_1}$.

6.7. (Coordinate Geometry) Equation of a Line (Slope-Intercept Form)
$y = mx + b$, m is the slope and b is the y-intercept.
$y = m(x - d)$, m is the slope and d is the x-intercept.

6.8. (Coordinate Geometry) Equation of a Line (Slope-Point Form)
$y - y_0 = m(x - x_0)$; (x_0, y_0) is the point and m is the slope.

6.9. (Coordinate Geometry) Equation of a Line (Intercept Form)
$\frac{x}{a} + \frac{y}{b} = 1$; intercepts a and b are on x axis and y axis respectively.

6.10. (Coordinate Geometry) Equation of a Line (Two Points Form)
$\frac{y - y_1}{x - x_1} = \frac{y_2 - y_1}{x_2 - x_1}$; (x_1, y_1) and (x_2, y_2) are two points on the line.

6.11. (Coordinate Geometry) Distance from a Point to a Line
For a line $Ax + By + C = 0$ and a point (x_1, y_1), the distance d is:

$$d = \frac{|Ax_1 + By_1 + C|}{\sqrt{A^2 + B^2}}.$$

6.12. (Coordinate Geometry) Distance between two Parallel Lines
For two lines $Ax + By + C_1$ and $Ax + By + C_2$, the distance d is:
$$\frac{|C_1 - C_2|}{\sqrt{A^2 + B^2}}.$$

6.13. (Coordinate Geometry) Angle Between two Lines
$$\theta = \tan^{-1}\left|\frac{m_2 - m_1}{1 + m_1 m_2}\right|,$$
Where m_1 = slope of line 1 & m_2 = slope of line 2

6.14. (Coordinate Geometry) Parallel Lines & Perpendicular Lines Equation
I. If one line is: $A_1 x + B_1 y + C_1 = 0$, a parallel line would have the same coefficients for x and y: $A_1 x + B_1 y + C_2 = 0$, the constant term C can be different.
II. If one line is: $A_1 x + B_1 y + C_1 = 0$, a line perpendicular to it would have coefficients such that: $A_1 = B_2$ and $B_1 = -A_2$

6.15. (Coordinate Geometry) Normal Form of a Line
$x \cos \theta + y \sin \theta = p$
Where θ is the angle that the perpendicular from the origin to the line makes with the positive x-axis.

p is the length of the perpendicular from the origin to the line.

6.16. (Coordinate Geometry) Centroid, Circumcenter, Orthocenter, Incenter of a Triangle

The triangle's vertices $(x_1, y_1), (x_2, y_2), (x_3, y_3)$

$$Centroid(G) = \left(\frac{x_1 + x_2 + x_3}{3}, \frac{y_1 + y_2 + y_3}{3}\right)$$

$Circumcenter(O) =$
$$\left(\frac{(x_1^2 + y_1^2)(y_2 - y_3) + (x_2^2 + y_2^2)(y_3 - y_1) + (x_3^2 + y_3^2)(y_1 - y_2)}{2(x_1(y_2 - y_3) + x_2(y_3 - y_1) + x_3(y_1 - y_2))},\right.$$
$$\left.\frac{(x_1^2 + y_1^2)(x_3 - x_2) + (x_2^2 + y_2^2)(x_1 - x_3) + (x_3^2 + y_3^2)(x_2 - x_1)}{2(x_1(y_2 - y_3) + x_2(y_3 - y_1) + x_3(y_1 - y_2))}\right)$$

Orthocenter $(H) =$
- Find the equations of two altitudes.
- Solve for their intersection.

$Incenter(I) =$
$$\left(\frac{\left(\sqrt{(x_2 - x_3)^2 + (y_2 - y_3)^2}\right)x_1 + \left(\sqrt{(x_3 - x_1)^2 + (y_3 - y_1)^2}\right)x_2 + \left(\sqrt{(x_1 - x_2)^2 + (y_1 - y_2)^2}\right)x_3}{\sqrt{(x_2 - x_3)^2 + (y_2 - y_3)^2} + \sqrt{(x_3 - x_1)^2 + (y_3 - y_1)^2} + \sqrt{(x_1 - x_2)^2 + (y_1 - y_2)^2}},\right.$$
$$\left.\frac{\left(\sqrt{(x_2 - x_3)^2 + (y_2 - y_3)^2}\right)y_1 + \left(\sqrt{(x_3 - x_1)^2 + (y_3 - y_1)^2}\right)y_2 + \left(\sqrt{(x_1 - x_2)^2 + (y_1 - y_2)^2}\right)y_3}{\sqrt{(x_2 - x_3)^2 + (y_2 - y_3)^2} + \sqrt{(x_3 - x_1)^2 + (y_3 - y_1)^2} + \sqrt{(x_1 - x_2)^2 + (y_1 - y_2)^2}}\right)$$

6.17. (Coordinate Geometry) Specific Conic Section and their Standard Forms

Circles: A circle is a special case of an ellipse where two foci coincide. Its general form is:
$(x - h)^2 + (y - k)^2 = r^2$; (h, k) is the center and r is the radius.

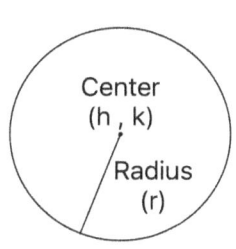

PROBLEMS IN SCHOOL MATHEMATICS

Ellipse: *An ellipse is defined by the equation:*
$\frac{(x-h)^2}{a^2} + \frac{(y-k)^2}{b^2} = 1$, *where (h, k) is the center, a is the semi-major axis, and b is the semi-minor axis. For $a > b$, the ellipse is elongated horizontally; for $a < b$, it is elongated vertically.*

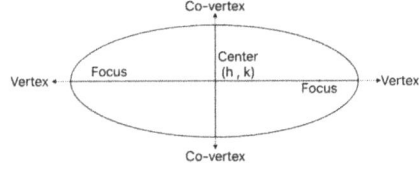

Parabola: *A parabola is defined by:* $y = ax^2 + bx + c$ *or, in its vertex form:* $y = a(x - h)^2 + k$ *or* $x = a(y - k)^2 + h$; (h, k) *is the vertex of the parabola.*

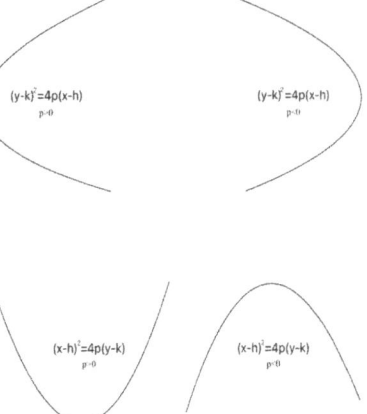

PROBLEMS IN SCHOOL MATHEMATICS

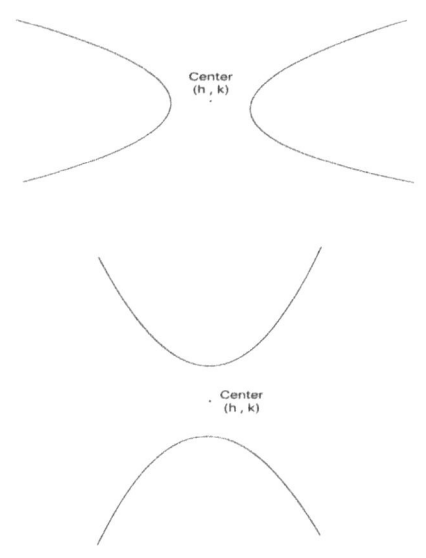

Hyperbola: *A hyperbola has the form:*

$$\frac{(x-h)^2}{a^2} - \frac{(y-k)^2}{b^2} = 1$$

or,

$$\frac{(y-k)^2}{a^2} - \frac{(x-h)^2}{b^2} = 1,$$

where (h, k) is the center, and a and b are real numbers that determine the shape and orientation of the hyperbola.

General Conic Section Equation:

$Ax^2 + Bxy + Cy^2 + Dx + Ey + F = 0$, *where A, B, C, D, E and F are constants.*

Depending on the values of A, B and C, the conic can be defined as:

Circle: $A = C$ *and* $B = 0$

Ellipse $(B^2 - 4AC < 0)$: $A \neq C, B = 0$ *and* $A > 0, C > 0$

Parabola $(B^2 - 4AC = 0)$: *Either* $A = 0$ *or* $C = 0$

Hyperbola $(B^2 - 4AC > 0)$: $A.C < 0$

Conic Section	Eccentricity $e = \dfrac{distance\ to focus}{distance\ to\ directri.}$	Foci	Symmetry
Circle	$e = 0$	Center acts like focus	Symmetric about x-axis and y-axis (Infinite symmetry lines)
Ellipse	$0 < e < 1$	Two foci along major axis	Symmetric about x-axis, y-axis and major axis
Parabola	$e = 1$	One focus	Symmetric about the axis of symmetry (Line through vertex and focus)
Hyperbola	$e > 1$	Two foci along transverse axis	Symmetric about x-axis, y-axis and asymptotes

Definitions of Key Terms in Conic Sections

➤ **Major Axis:** The major axis is the longest line passing through the center, vertices, and foci of an ellipse. Its length is $2a$, where a is the semi-major axis.

➤ **Minor Axis:** The minor axis is the shortest line passing through the center and perpendicular to the major axis of an ellipse. Its length is $2b$, where b is the semi-minor axis.

➤ **Transverse Axis:** The transverse axis is the segment joining the two vertices of hyperbola. It correspond the major axis in an ellipse.

➤ **Conjugate Axis:** The conjugate axis is the line segment perpendicular to the transverse axis and passing through the center of a hyperbola.

➤ **Asymptotes:** The asymptotes are the straight lines that the hyperbola approaches but never touches. These lines pass through the center and intersect the conjugate and transverse axes.

- **Horizontal Hyperbola:** $y = \pm \frac{b}{a} x$
- **Vertical Hyperbola:** $y = \pm \frac{a}{b} x$

➤ **Latus Rectum:** The latus rectum is a line segment passing through a focus and perpendicular to the axis of symmetry.

- **Parabola:** $4p$, where p is the distance from the vertex to the focus.

- **Ellipse and Hyperbola:** $\frac{2b^2}{a}$, where a and b are the semi-major and semi-minor axes.

➢ **Vertices:** The vertices are the points where the conic section intersects its major or transverse axis.
  - **Ellipse:** Two vertices on the major axis.
  - **Hyperbola:** Two vertices on the transverse axis.
  - **Parabola:** One vertex, the point where the parabola is closest to its directrix and where it changes direction.

➢ **Co-Vertices:** The co-vertices are the endpoints of the minor axis of an ellipse or the conjugate axis of a hyperbola. Located at $(h, k \pm b)$ or $(h \pm b, k)$, depending on orientation.

➢ **Focus (Foci):** The focus (plural foci) is a fixed point (or points) that determine the shape of conic section.
  - **Ellipse:** Two foci inside the ellipse. The sum of distances from any point on the ellipse to the two foci is constant.
  - **Hyperbola:** Two foci outside the hyperbola. The difference of distances from any point on the hyperbola to the two foci is constant.
  - **Parabola:** One focus. The distance from any point on the parabola to the focus equals its distance to the directrix.

- **Directrix:** *The directrix is a fixed line that, along with focus, defines a conic section.*
  - **Parabola:** *A point's distance to the focus equals its perpendicular distance to the directrix.*
  - **Ellipse and Hyperbola:** *The directrix is related to the eccentricity and is positioned perpendicular to the major axis.*
- **Eccentricity (e):** *The eccentricity is a measure of how much a conic section deviates from being circular.*
  - *Circle:* $e = 0$
  - *Ellipse:* $0 < e < 1$
  - *Parabola:* $e = 1$
  - *Hyperbola:* $e > 1$
- **Center:** *The center is the midpoint of the line segment joining the foci of a conic section. It acts as a point of symmetry for the figure.*
  - *For ellipse and hyperbola, the center is the midpoint of the major and minor axes (ellipse) or transverse and conjugate axes (hyperbola).*
  - *For a parabola, the center is not defined because it has only one focus.*
- **Radii (or Radius):** *The radius is commonly used to describe the distance from the center to any point on a circle. For other conic sections, this term is not standard.*

6.18. (Coordinate Geometry) Three Dimensional Coordinate Geometry

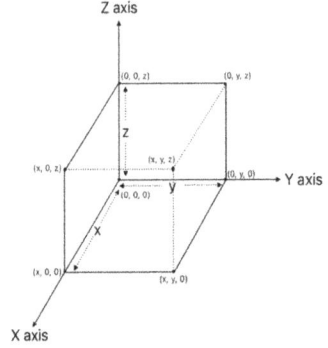

Coordinate on X axis $(x, 0, 0)$
Coordinate on Y axis $(0, y, 0)$
Coordinate on Z axis $(0, 0, z)$
Point on XY plane $(x, y, 0)$
Point on YZ plane $(0, y, z)$
Point on ZX plane $(x, 0, z)$

Distance between Two Points:
If the points are $A(x_1, y_1, z_1)$ and $B(x_2, y_2, z_2)$, the distance between them is given by:
$$AB = \sqrt{(x_2 - x_1)^2 + (y_2 - y_1)^2 + (z_2 - z_1)^2}.$$

The Signs of the Coordinates in each Octant:

Octant	Sign of x	Sign of y	Sign of z
1	+	+	+
2	−	+	+
3	−	−	+
4	+	−	+
5	+	+	−
6	−	+	−
7	−	−	−
8	+	−	−

Section Formula:

If a point $P(x, y, z)$ divides the line segment joining points $A(x_1, y_1, z_1)$ and $B(x_2, y_2, z_2)$ in the ratio $m:n$, the coordinates of P are:

$$P\left(\frac{mx_2 + nx_1}{m+n}, \frac{my_2 + ny_1}{m+n}, \frac{mz_2 + nz_1}{m+n}\right).$$

Midpoint Formula:

If $A(x_1, y_1, z_1)$ and $B(x_2, y_2, z_2)$ are two points, the midpoint M of the line segment joining them is:

$M\left(\frac{x_1+x_2}{2}, \frac{y_1+y_2}{2}, \frac{z_1+z_2}{2}\right).$

Area of Triangle

With Vertices $(x_1, y_1, z_1), (x_2, y_2, z_2)$ & (x_3, y_3, z_3) is:

$\frac{1}{2}\sqrt{[(y_2-y_1)(z_3-z_1)-(z_2-z_1)(y_3-y_1)]^2 + [(z_2-z_1)(x_3-x_1)-(x_2-x_1)(z_3-z_1)]^2 + [(x_2-x_1)(y_3-y_1)-(y_2-y_1)(x_3-x_1)]^2}$

Direction Cosines and Direction Ratios:

If a line has direction ratios a, b, c then the direction cosines l, m, n are given by:

$$l = \frac{a}{\sqrt{a^2+b^2+c^2}}, m = \frac{b}{\sqrt{a^2+b^2+c^2}},$$
$$n = \frac{c}{\sqrt{a^2+b^2+c^2}}$$

and $l^2 + m^2 + n^2 = 1$

Equation of a Line in 3D:

Vector Form: The equation of a line passing through a point $A(x_1, y_1, z_1)$ and parallel to a vector $\vec{b} = \langle a, b, c \rangle$ is:

$\vec{r} = \vec{a} + \lambda \vec{b}$

Where $\vec{r} = \langle x, y, z \rangle$ and $\vec{a} = \langle x_1, y_1, z_1 \rangle$, λ is a scalar.

Cartesian Form:
The Cartesian equation of a line passing through (x_1, y_1, z_1) and having direction ratios a, b, c is:
$$\frac{x - x_1}{a} = \frac{y - y_1}{b} = \frac{z - z_1}{c}$$

Equation of a Plane in 3D:

General Form:
The general equation of a plane is:
$$ax + by + cz + d = 0$$
Where a, b, c are the direction ratios of the normal to the plane.

Normal Form:
The equation of a plane at a distance d from the origin and having a unit normal vector $\hat{n} = \langle l, m, n \rangle$ is:
$$lx + my + nz = d$$

Angle between Two Lines:
If two lines have direction cosines (l_1, m_1, n_1) and (l_2, m_2, n_2), the angle θ between the lines is:
$$\cos\theta = l_1 l_2 + m_1 m_2 + n_1 n_2$$

Angle between Two Planes:
If two planes have normal $\vec{n_1} = \langle a_1, b_1, c_1 \rangle$ and $\vec{n_2} = \langle a_2, b_2, c_2 \rangle$, the angle θ between the planes is:
$$\cos\theta = \frac{a_1 a_2 + b_1 b_2 + c_1 c_2}{\sqrt{a_1^2 + b_1^2 + c_1^2} \cdot \sqrt{a_2^2 + b_2^2 + c_2^2}}$$

Angle between a Line and a Plane:
The angle θ between a line with direction ratios a, b, c and a plane with normal $a_1 x + b_1 y + c_1 z = 0$ is:
$$\sin\theta = \frac{|a a_1 + b b_1 + c c_1|}{\sqrt{a^2 + b^2 + c^2} \cdot \sqrt{a_1^2 + b_1^2 + c_1^2}}$$

PROBLEMS IN SCHOOL MATHEMATICS

Shortest Distance between Two Skew Lines:

If two lines are given by:

$$\frac{x-x_1}{a_1} = \frac{y-y_1}{b_1} = \frac{z-z_1}{c_1}$$

$$\frac{x-x_2}{a_2} = \frac{y-y_2}{b_2} = \frac{z-z_2}{c_2}$$

The shortest distance d between them is:

$$d = \frac{|(x_2-x_1)(b_1c_2-b_2c_1) + (y_2-y_1)(c_1a_2-c_2a_1) + (z_2-z_1)(a_1b_2-a_2b_1)|}{\sqrt{(b_1c_2-b_2c_1)^2 + (c_1a_2-c_2a_1)^2 + (a_1b_2-a_2b_1)^2}}$$

PROBLEMS IN SCHOOL MATHEMATICS

Problems

Coordinate Geometry (Straight Lines) 1
Find the area of the closed region bounded by the equation $|x| + |y| = 10$, in the two dimensional plane?
Hint

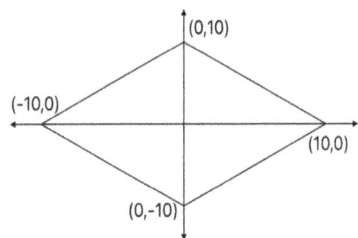

Coordinate Geometry (Straight Lines) 2
(0,0,0), (a,0,0), (0,b,0) and (0,0,c) are four distinct points, what are the coordinates of the point which is equidistant from the four points?
Hint
Coordinates of the points
$$= \left(\frac{0+a+0+0}{2}, \frac{0+0+b+0}{2}, \frac{0+0+0+c}{2}\right)$$

Coordinate Geometry (Straight Lines) 3
Find the area of triangle with vertices $(a, b + c - a), (b, c + a - b), (c, a + b - c)$.

PROBLEMS IN SCHOOL MATHEMATICS

Hint

Area of triangle
$$=\frac{1}{2}[a\{(c+a-b)-(a+b-c)\}+b\{(a+b-c)-(b+c-a)\}+c\{(b+c-a)-(c+a-b)\}]$$

Coordinate Geometry (Straight Lines) 4

Show that the reciprocal of the length of perpendicular from the origin on the line $\frac{x}{a}+\frac{y}{b}=1$ is $\sqrt{\frac{1}{a^2}+\frac{1}{b^2}}$.

Hint

Reciprocal of perpendicular $= \dfrac{1}{\dfrac{1}{\sqrt{\dfrac{1}{a^2}+\dfrac{1}{b^2}}}}$

Coordinate Geometry (Straight Lines) 5

Show that the tangent of an angle between the lines $bx+ay=100ab$ and $bx-ay=50ab$ is $\frac{2ab}{a^2-b^2}$.

Hint

$bx+ay=100ab$, $Slope(m_1)=-\frac{b}{a}$

$bx-ay=50ab$, $Slope(m_2)=\frac{b}{a}$

Coordinate Geometry (Straight Lines) 6

Show that the equation of a line passing through $(k\sin^{101}\theta, k\cos^{101}\theta)$ and perpendicular to the line $x\csc^{99}\theta+y\sec^{99}\theta=m$ is

$x \sin^{99}\theta - y\cos^{99}\theta$
$$= k[(\sin^{100}\theta + \cos^{100}\theta)(\sin^{50}\theta + \cos^{50}\theta)(\sin^{25}\theta + \cos^{25}\theta)(\sin^{25}\theta - \cos^{25}\theta)]$$

Hint
Line perpendicular to the line $x\csc^{99}\theta + y\sec^{99}\theta = m$
is $x\sec^{99}\theta - y\csc^{99}\theta + n = 0$
$\therefore k\sin^{101}\theta \times \sec^{99}\theta - k\cos^{101}\theta \times \csc^{99}\theta + n = 0$
$Or, n = k(\cos^{101}\theta \csc^{99}\theta - \sin^{101}\theta \sec^{99}\theta)$
$\therefore x\sec^{99}\theta - y\csc^{99}\theta$
$$+ k(\cos^{101}\theta \csc^{99}\theta - \sin^{101}\theta \sec^{99}\theta) = 0$$
$Or, \dfrac{x}{\cos^{99}\theta} - \dfrac{y}{\sin^{99}\theta} + k\left(\dfrac{\cos^{101}\theta}{\sin^{99}\theta} - \dfrac{\sin^{101}\theta}{\cos^{99}\theta}\right) = 0$
$Or, x\sin^{99}\theta - y\cos^{99}\theta + k(\cos^{101}\theta \times \cos^{99}\theta - \sin^{101}\theta \times \sin^{99}\theta) = 0$

Coordinate Geometry (Conic Sections) 7
If two circles $x^2 + y^2 + 2g_1x + 2f_1y = 0$ *and*
$x^2 + y^2 + 2g_2x + 2f_2y = 0$ *touch each other, and then prove that* $f_1g_2 = f_2g_1$.

Hint
Distance between their centres
= Sum or difference of their radii
$Or, \sqrt{(g_1-g_2)^2 + (f_1-f_2)^2} = \sqrt{(g_1^2+f_1^2)} \pm \sqrt{g_2^2+f_2^2}$

Coordinate Geometry (Conic Sections) 8
A right angle triangle is inscribed in the parabola

$x^2 = 4ay$, right angle of a triangle is the vertex of the parabola. Find the lengths of the sides of the triangle?

Hint

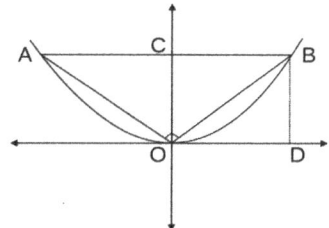

$\angle AOB = 90°$, $\angle BOC = \angle AOC = 45°$

$\cos 45° = \frac{OC}{OB}$, $\sin 45° = \frac{BC}{OB}$

Therefore, $OC = \frac{OB}{\sqrt{2}}$, $BC = \frac{OB}{\sqrt{2}}$

So, $OC = BD = OD = BC = \frac{OB}{\sqrt{2}}$

Coordinates of $B = \left(\frac{OB}{\sqrt{2}}, \frac{OB}{\sqrt{2}}\right)$

$\left(\frac{OB}{\sqrt{2}}, \frac{OB}{\sqrt{2}}\right)$ will satisfy $x^2 = 4ay$

Or, $\left(\frac{OB}{\sqrt{2}}\right)^2 = 4 \times a \times \frac{OB}{\sqrt{2}}$

$\therefore OB = 4\sqrt{2}a$

Similarly, $OA = 4\sqrt{2}a$

Applying Pythagoras theorem
$$(AB)^2 = (OA)^2 + (OB)^2$$

Coordinate Geometry (Three Dimensions) 9

If l_1, m_1, n_1; l_2, m_2, n_2; l_3, m_3, n_3 are the direction cosines of three mutually perpendicular lines, prove that the line whose direction cosines are proportional to

PROBLEMS IN SCHOOL MATHEMATICS

$l_1 + l_2 + l_3, m_1 + m_2 + m_3, n_1 + n_2 + n_3$ *makes equal angles with them.*

Hint

Let three angles be θ_1, θ_2 *and* θ_3 *respectively.*

$$\cos\theta_1 = \frac{l_1(l_1+l_2+l_3) + m_1(m_1+m_2+m_3) + n_1(n_1+n_2+n_3)}{\sqrt{(l_1^2+m_1^2+n_1^2)}\sqrt{(l_1+l_2+l_3)^2 + (m_1+m_2+m_3)^2 + (n_1+n_2+n_3)^2}}$$

$$\cos\theta_2 = \frac{l_2(l_1+l_2+l_3) + m_2(m_1+m_2+m_3) + n_2(n_1+n_2+n_3)}{\sqrt{(l_2^2+m_2^2+n_2^2)}\sqrt{(l_1+l_2+l_3)^2 + (m_1+m_2+m_3)^2 + (n_1+n_2+n_3)^2}}$$

$$\cos\theta_3 = \frac{l_3(l_1+l_2+l_3) + m_3(m_1+m_2+m_3) + n_3(n_1+n_2+n_3)}{\sqrt{(l_3^2+m_3^2+n_3^2)}\sqrt{(l_1+l_2+l_3)^2 + (m_1+m_2+m_3)^2 + (n_1+n_2+n_3)^2}}$$

Coordinate Geometry (Three Dimensions) 10

If a variable line in two adjacent positions has direction cosines l, m, n *and* $l + \delta l, m + \delta m, n + \delta n$, *show that small angles* $\delta\theta$ *between two positions is given by*
$(\delta\theta)^2 = (\delta l)^2 + (\delta m)^2 + (\delta n)^2$.

Hint

$(l + \delta l)^2 + (m + \delta m)^2 + (n + \delta n)^2 = 1$

$Or, (l^2 + m^2 + n^2) + 2(l\delta l + m\delta m + n\delta n) + (\delta l)^2 + (\delta m)^2 + (\delta n)^2 = 1$

$\therefore l\delta l + m\delta m + n\delta n = -\frac{1}{2}\{(\delta l)^2 + (\delta m)^2 + (\delta n)^2\}$

Because $l^2 + m^2 + n^2 = 1$

$\therefore \cos\delta\theta = l(l + \delta l) + m(m + \delta m) + n(n + \delta n)$

$Or, \cos\delta\theta = 1 - \frac{1}{2}\{(\delta l)^2 + (\delta m)^2 + (\delta n)^2\}$

$Or, 2 \times 2 \sin^2\frac{\delta\theta}{2} = (\delta l)^2 + (\delta m)^2 + (\delta n)^2$

$\left[\frac{\delta\theta}{2} \text{ is small, so } \sin\frac{\delta\theta}{2} = \frac{\delta\theta}{2}\right]$

TRIGONOMETRY

7. Trigonometry
Trigonometry is the branch of mathematics that studies the relationships between the angles and the sides of triangles.

7.1. (Trigonometry) Degree and Radian Relationship
Degrees: A degree is a unit of angle measurement where full circle is divided into 360 equal parts.
Radians: A radian is measure of angle based on the radius of circle. One radian is the angle created when the arc length is equal to the radius of the circle. A full circle is radians is 2π, which is approximately 6.2832 radians.

$$Radians = Degrees \times \frac{\pi}{180}$$
$$Degrees = Radians \times \frac{180}{\pi}$$

7.2. (Trigonometry) Trigonometric Ratios
For an angle θ in a right triangle,

$Sine(sin): sin(\theta) = \frac{Opposite\ Side}{Hypotenuse}$

$sin(\theta) = \frac{e^{i\theta} - e^{-i\theta}}{2i}$ (for complex numbers)

$Cosine(cos): cos(\theta) = \frac{Adjacent\ Side}{Hypotenuse}$

$cos(\theta) = \frac{e^{i\theta} + e^{-i\theta}}{2}$ (for complex numbers)

$$Tangent(tan): tan(\theta) = \frac{Opposite\ Side}{Adjacent\ Side}$$

$$Cotangent(cot): cot(\theta) = \frac{1}{tan(\theta)}$$

$$Secant(sec): sec(\theta) = \frac{1}{cos(\theta)}$$

$$Cosecant(cosec): cosec(\theta) = \frac{1}{sin(\theta)}$$

7.3. (Trigonometry) Law of Sines
For any triangle with angles A, B and C and opposite sides a, b and c respectively:
$$\frac{a}{sin\ A} = \frac{b}{sin\ B} = \frac{c}{sin\ C}$$

7.4. (Trigonometry) Law of Cosines
For any triangle with sides a, b and c and angle C opposite side c:
$$c^2 = a^2 + b^2 - 2ab\ cos\ C$$

7.5. (Trigonometry) Euler's Formula
$$e^{i\theta} = cos(\theta) + i\ sin(\theta)$$

7.6. (Trigonometry) Pythagorean Identities
$$sin^2(\theta) + cos^2(\theta) = 1$$
$$1 + tan^2(\theta) = sec^2(\theta)$$
$$1 + cot^2(\theta) = cosec^2(\theta)$$

7.7. (Trigonometry) Expressing each Trigonometric Ratio in Terms of each Others

	$sin(\theta)$	$cos(\theta)$	$tan(\theta)$	$cot(\theta)$	$sec(\theta)$	$cosec(\theta)$
$sin\theta$	$sin\theta$	$\sqrt{1-cos^2\theta}$	$\dfrac{tan\theta}{\sqrt{1+tan^2\theta}}$	$\dfrac{1}{\sqrt{1+cot^2\theta}}$	$\dfrac{\sqrt{sec^2\theta-1}}{sec\theta}$	$\dfrac{1}{cosec\theta}$
$cos\theta$	$\sqrt{1-sin^2\theta}$	$cos\theta$	$\dfrac{1}{\sqrt{1+tan^2\theta}}$	$\dfrac{cot\theta}{\sqrt{1+cot^2\theta}}$	$\dfrac{1}{sec\theta}$	$\dfrac{\sqrt{cosec^2\theta-1}}{cosec\theta}$
$tan\theta$	$\dfrac{sin\theta}{\sqrt{1-sin^2\theta}}$	$\dfrac{\sqrt{1-cos^2\theta}}{cos\theta}$	$tan\theta$	$\dfrac{1}{cot\theta}$	$\sqrt{sec^2\theta-1}$	$\dfrac{1}{\sqrt{cosec^2\theta-1}}$
$cot\theta$	$\dfrac{\sqrt{1-sin^2\theta}}{sin\theta}$	$\dfrac{cos\theta}{\sqrt{1-cos^2\theta}}$	$\dfrac{1}{tan\theta}$	$cot\theta$	$\dfrac{1}{\sqrt{sec^2\theta-1}}$	$\sqrt{cosec^2\theta-1}$
$sec\theta$	$\dfrac{1}{\sqrt{1-sin^2\theta}}$	$\dfrac{1}{cos\theta}$	$\sqrt{1+tan^2\theta}$	$\dfrac{\sqrt{1+cot^2\theta}}{cot\theta}$	$sec\theta$	$\dfrac{cosec\theta}{\sqrt{cosec^2\theta-1}}$
$cosec\theta$	$\dfrac{1}{sin\theta}$	$\dfrac{1}{\sqrt{1-cos^2\theta}}$	$\dfrac{\sqrt{1+tan^2\theta}}{tan\theta}$	$\sqrt{1+cot^2\theta}$	$\dfrac{sec\theta}{\sqrt{sec^2\theta-1}}$	$cosec\theta$

7.8. (Trigonometry) Angle Sum and Difference Formulas

$sin(A+B) = sin A \cos B + \cos A \sin B$

$cos(A+B) = \cos A \cos B - \sin A \sin B$

$tan(A+B) = \dfrac{\tan A + \tan B}{1 - \tan A \tan B}$

$cot(A+B) = \dfrac{\cot A \cot B - 1}{\cot B + \cot A}$

$sin(A-B) = \sin A \cos B - \cos A \sin B$

$cos(A-B) = \cos A \cos B + \sin A \sin B$

$tan(A-B) = \dfrac{\tan A - \tan B}{1 + \tan A \tan B}$

$cot(A-B) = \dfrac{\cot A \cot B + 1}{\cot B - \cot A}$

7.9. (Trigonometry) Converting Product into Sum/Difference and Vice Versa

$2 \sin A \cos B = \sin(A + B) + \sin(A - B)$

$2 \cos A \sin B = \sin(A + B) - \sin(A - B)$

$2 \cos A \cos B = \cos(A + B) + \cos(A - B)$

$-2 \sin A \sin B = \cos(A + B) - \cos(A - B)$

$\sin A + \sin B = 2 \sin\left(\dfrac{A+B}{2}\right) \cos\left(\dfrac{A-B}{2}\right)$

$\sin A - \sin B = 2 \cos\left(\dfrac{A+B}{2}\right) \sin\left(\dfrac{A-B}{2}\right)$

$\cos A + \cos B = 2 \cos\left(\dfrac{A+B}{2}\right) \cos\left(\dfrac{A-B}{2}\right)$

$\cos A - \cos B = -2 \sin\left(\dfrac{A+B}{2}\right) \sin\left(\dfrac{A-B}{2}\right)$

7.10. (Trigonometry) Double Angle Formulas

$\sin(2\theta) = 2 \sin\theta \cos\theta = \dfrac{2 \tan\theta}{1 + \tan^2\theta}$

$\cos(2\theta) = \cos^2\theta - \sin^2\theta = 2\cos^2\theta - 1 = 1 - 2\sin^2\theta$

$= \dfrac{1 - \tan^2\theta}{1 + \tan^2\theta}$

$\tan(2\theta) = \dfrac{2 \tan\theta}{1 - \tan^2\theta}$

7.11. (Trigonometry) Triple Angle Formulas

$\sin(3\theta) = 3 \sin\theta - 4 \sin^3\theta$

$\cos(3\theta) = 4 \cos^3\theta - 3 \cos\theta$

$\tan(3\theta) = \dfrac{3 \tan\theta - \tan^3\theta}{1 - 3 \tan^2\theta}$

7.12. (Trigonometry) Basic Trigonometric Values for Common Angles

Angle (°)	$\sin(\theta)$	$\cos(\theta)$	$\tan(\theta)$	$\cot(\theta)$	$\sec(\theta)$	$\csc(\theta)$
0°	0	1	0	∞	1	∞
30°	$\dfrac{1}{2}$	$\dfrac{\sqrt{3}}{2}$	$\dfrac{1}{\sqrt{3}}$	$\sqrt{3}$	$\dfrac{2}{\sqrt{3}}$	2
45°	$\dfrac{1}{\sqrt{2}}$	$\dfrac{1}{\sqrt{2}}$	1	1	$\sqrt{2}$	$\sqrt{2}$
60°	$\dfrac{\sqrt{3}}{2}$	$\dfrac{1}{2}$	$\sqrt{3}$	$\dfrac{1}{\sqrt{3}}$	2	$\dfrac{2}{\sqrt{3}}$
90°	1	0	∞	0	∞	1
180°	0	−1	0	∞	−1	∞
270°	−1	0	∞	0	∞	−1
360°	0	1	0	∞	1	∞

7.13. (Trigonometry) Signs of Trigonometric Functions

First Quadrant (0° to 90°)

Sine(sin): Positive
Cosine(cos): Positive
Tangent(tan): Positive

Second Quadrant (90° to 180°)

Sine(sin): Positive
Cosine(cos): Negative
Tangent(tan): Negative

Third Quadrant (180° to 270°)

Sine(sin): Negative
Cosine(cos): Negative
Tangent(tan): Positive

Fourth Quadrant(270° to 360°)
Sine(sin): Negative
Cosine(cos): Positive
Tangent(tan): Negative

7.14. (Trigonometry) ASTC Rule
All trigonometric functions are positive in the first quadrant.
Sine is positive in the second quadrant.
Tangent is positive in the third quadrant.
Cosine is positive in the fourth quadrant.

7.15. (Trigonometry) Periodicity
Trigonometric functions change as the angle varies within different quadrants and across different periods.

Sine and Cosine: *Period of 360° or 2π radians. They repeat every 360° or 2π radians.*

Tangent and Cotangent: *Period of 180° or π radians. They repeat every 180° or π radians.*

7.16. (Trigonometry) The Classification of Functions as Odd and Even
Odd Functions: $\sin(x), \tan(x), \cot(x), \csc(x)$
For those functions, $f(-x) = -f(x)$
Even Functions: $\cos(x), \sec(x)$
For those functions, $f(-x) = f(x)$

7.17. (Trigonometry) Allied Angles
Sine Function (sin)
$\sin(90° \pm \theta) = \cos(\theta)$
$\sin(180° \pm \theta) = \pm \sin(\theta)$
$\sin(270° \pm \theta) = -\cos(\theta)$
$\sin(360° \pm \theta) = \pm \sin(\theta)$
Cosine Function (cos)
$\cos(90° \pm \theta) = \mp \sin(\theta)$
$\cos(180° \pm \theta) = -\cos(\theta)$
$\cos(270° \pm \theta) = \pm \sin(\theta)$
$\cos(360° \pm \theta) = \cos(\theta)$
Tangent Function (tan)
$\tan(90° \pm \theta) = \mp \cot(\theta)$
$\tan(180° \pm \theta) = \pm \tan(\theta)$
$\tan(270° \pm \theta) = \mp \cot(\theta)$
$\tan(360° \pm \theta) = \pm \tan(\theta)$
Cotangent Function (cot)
$\cot(90° \pm \theta) = \mp \tan(\theta)$
$\cot(180° \pm \theta) = \pm \cot(\theta)$
$\cot(270° \pm \theta) = \mp \tan(\theta)$
$\cot(360° \pm \theta) = \pm \cot(\theta)$
Secant Function (sec)
$\sec(90° \pm \theta) = \mp \csc(\theta)$
$\sec(180° \pm \theta) = -\sec(\theta)$
$\sec(270° \pm \theta) = \pm \csc(\theta)$
$\sec(360° \pm \theta) = \sec(\theta)$

Cosecant Function (cosec)
$cosec(90° \pm \theta) = sec(\theta)$
$cosec(180° \pm \theta) = \pm cosec(\theta)$
$cosec(270° \pm \theta) = -sec(\theta)$
$cosec(360° \pm \theta) = \pm cosec(\theta)$

7.18. (Trigonometry) Inverse Trigonometric Functions
Arcsine(sin^{-1} or asin)
Domain: $[-1, 1]$
Range: $\left[-\frac{\pi}{2}, \frac{\pi}{2}\right]$
Arccosine(cos^{-1} or acos)
Domain: $[-1, 1]$
Range: $[0, \pi]$
Arctangent(tan^{-1} or atan)
Domain: $(-\infty, \infty)$
Range: $\left(-\frac{\pi}{2}, \frac{\pi}{2}\right)$
Arccotangent(cot^{-1} or acot)
Domain: $(-\infty, \infty)$
Range: $(0, \pi)$
Arcsecant(sec^{-1} or asec)
Domain: $(-\infty, -1] \cup [1, \infty)$
Range: $\left[0, \frac{\pi}{2}\right) \cup \left(\frac{\pi}{2}, \pi\right]$
Arccosecant(cosec^{-1} or acosec)
Domain: $(-\infty, -1] \cup [1, \infty)$
Range: $\left[-\frac{\pi}{2}, 0\right) \cup \left(0, \frac{\pi}{2}\right]$

PROBLEMS IN SCHOOL MATHEMATICS

Simplification of Composite Functions:

$\sin(\arcsin(x)) = x$ for $-1 \leq x \leq 1$

$\cos(\arccos(x)) = x$ for $-1 \leq x \leq 1$

$\tan(\arctan(x)) = x$ for all $x \in \mathbb{R}$

$\arcsin(\sin(x)) = x$, if $-\dfrac{\pi}{2} \leq x \leq \dfrac{\pi}{2}$

$\arccos(\cos(x)) = x$, if $0 \leq x \leq \pi$

$\arctan(\tan(x)) = x$, if $-\dfrac{\pi}{2} \leq x \leq \dfrac{\pi}{2}$

$\sin(\arccos(x)) = \sqrt{1-x^2}$ for $-1 \leq x \leq 1$

$\cos(\arcsin(x)) = \sqrt{1-x^2}$ for $-1 \leq x \leq 1$

$\tan(\arcsin(x)) = \dfrac{x}{\sqrt{1-x^2}}$ for $-1 \leq x \leq 1$

$\sin(\arccos(x)) = \dfrac{\sqrt{1-x^2}}{x}$ for $0 \leq x \leq 1$

Addition & Subtraction Formulas:

$\arcsin(x) \pm \arcsin(y) = \arcsin\left(x\sqrt{1-y^2} \pm y\sqrt{1-x^2}\right)$

$\arccos(x) \pm \arccos(y)$
$\qquad = \arccos\left(xy \mp \sqrt{(1-x^2)(1-y^2)}\right)$

$\arctan(x) \pm \arctan(y)$
$= \begin{cases} \arctan\left(\dfrac{x \pm y}{1 \mp xy}\right), \text{ if } xy < 1 \\ \arctan\left(\dfrac{x \pm y}{1 \mp xy}\right) + \pi, \text{ if } xy \geq 1 \end{cases}$

$\arcsin(x) + \arccos(x) = \dfrac{\pi}{2}$

$\arctan(x) + \arctan\left(\dfrac{1}{x}\right) = \dfrac{\pi}{2}$, for $x > 0$

PROBLEMS IN SCHOOL MATHEMATICS

Symmetric Properties:
$arcsin(-x) = -arcsin(x)$
$arccos(-x) = \pi - arccos(x)$
$arctan(-x) = -arctan(x)$

7.19. (Trigonometry) General Solution of Trigonometric Equations

   I. $sin(x) = k$:
$x = arcsin(k) + 2n\pi$ Or $x = \pi - arcsin(k) + 2n\pi$, $n \in \mathbb{Z}$

   II. $cos(x) = k$:
$x = arccos(k) + 2n\pi$ Or $x = -arccos(k) + 2n\pi$, $n \in \mathbb{Z}$

   III. $tan(x) = k$:
$x = arctan(k) + n\pi$, $n \in \mathbb{Z}$

7.20. (Trigonometry) Applications

The angle of elevation and the angle of depression are concepts used in trigonometry to describe angles formed between a horizontal line and a line of sight. These concepts are often applied in problems involving height and distance.

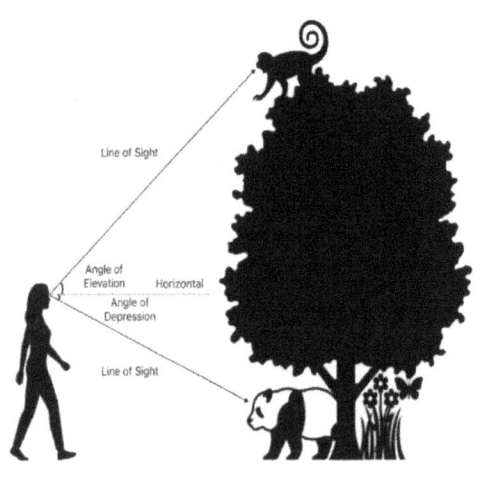

PROBLEMS IN SCHOOL MATHEMATICS

Problems

Trigonometry (Functions & Identities) 1
Prove that, $\sin^4\theta - \cos^4\theta + 1 = 2\sin^2\theta$.
Hint
$\sin^4\theta - \cos^4\theta + 1$
$= (\sin^2\theta)^2 - (\cos^2\theta)^2 + \sin^2\theta + \cos^2\theta$

Trigonometry (Functions & Identities) 2
If $\cot\theta - \cot^2\theta = 1$,
then show that, $\cosec^2\theta - \cosec^4\theta = 1$.
Hint
$\cot\theta - \cot^2\theta = 1$
Or, $\cot\theta = 1 + \cot^2\theta$
$\therefore \cot\theta = \cosec^2\theta$

Trigonometry (Functions & Identities) 3
Prove that, $\dfrac{\sin^3 A - \cos^3 A}{\sin A - \cos A} - \sin A \cos A = 1$.
Hint
$\dfrac{\sin^3 A - \cos^3 A}{\sin A - \cos A} - \sin A \cos A$
$= \dfrac{(\sin A - \cos A)(\sin^2 A + \sin A \cos A + \cos^2 A)}{(\sin A - \cos A)} - \sin A \cos A$

Trigonometry (Functions & Identities) 4
If $\tan x + \cot x = 2$,
then show that, $\tan^{100} x + \cot^{100} x = 2$.

Hint
$\tan x + \cot x = 2$
Or, $\tan x + \frac{1}{\tan x} = 2$
Or, $\tan^2 x - 2\tan x + 1 = 2$
Or, $(\tan x - 1)^2 = 0$
$\therefore \tan x = 1$

Trigonometry (Functions & Identities) 5
If $\tan \theta + \cot \theta = 2$, then show that,
$\sin \theta + \cos \theta = \pm \sqrt{2}$.

Hint
$\tan \theta + \cot \theta = 2$
Or, $\frac{\sin \theta}{\cos \theta} + \frac{\cos \theta}{\sin \theta} = 2$
Or, $\sin^2 \theta - 2\sin \theta \cos \theta + \cos^2 \theta = 0$
Or, $2 \sin \theta \cos \theta = 1$
Identity used, $\sin^2 \theta + \cos^2 \theta = 1$
Or, $\sin^2 \theta + 2 \sin \theta \cos \theta + \cos^2 \theta - 2 \sin \theta \cos \theta = 1$
Or, $(\sin \theta + \cos \theta)^2 - 2 \sin \theta \cos \theta = 1$
[Formula used; $a^2 + b^2 = (a + b)^2 - 2ab$, where $a = \sin \theta$ and $b = \cos \theta$]
Or, $(\sin \theta + \cos \theta)^2 - 1 = 1$, because $2 \sin \theta \cos \theta = 1$

Trigonometry (Functions & Identities) 6
If $\cosec x = 7$, $\frac{\pi}{2} < x < \pi$,
then show that, $\cot \frac{x}{2} = 7 - \sqrt{48}$.

Hint
$\sin x = \frac{1}{\cosec x}$, $\cos x = \pm\sqrt{1 - \sin^2 x}$,

$\cos x = 2\cos^2 \dfrac{x}{2} - 1$ or $1 - 2\sin^2 \dfrac{x}{2}$

Trigonometry (Functions & Identities) 7
Prove that, $2\cos\dfrac{39\pi}{101}\cos\dfrac{41\pi}{101} + \cos\dfrac{21\pi}{101} + \cos\dfrac{99\pi}{101} = 0$.

Hint

$2\cos\dfrac{39\pi}{101}\cos\dfrac{41\pi}{101} + \cos\dfrac{21\pi}{101} + \cos\dfrac{99\pi}{101}$

$= \cos\left(\dfrac{39\pi}{101} + \dfrac{41\pi}{101}\right) + \cos\left(\dfrac{39\pi}{101} - \dfrac{41\pi}{101}\right) + \cos\dfrac{21\pi}{101} + \cos\dfrac{99\pi}{101}$

$= \cos\dfrac{80\pi}{101} + \cos\dfrac{2\pi}{101} + \cos\dfrac{21\pi}{101} + \cos\dfrac{99\pi}{101}$

$= \left(\cos\dfrac{80\pi}{101} + \cos\dfrac{21\pi}{101}\right)\left(\cos\dfrac{99\pi}{101} + \cos\dfrac{2\pi}{101}\right)$

Trigonometry (Functions & Identities) 8
Prove that, $\dfrac{\sin 70° - \sin 40°}{\cos 70° + \cos 40°} = 2 - \sqrt{3}$.

Hint

$\dfrac{\sin 70° - \sin 40°}{\cos 70° + \cos 40°} = \dfrac{2\cos\dfrac{70°+40°}{2}\sin\dfrac{70°-40°}{2}}{2\cos\dfrac{70°+40°}{2}\cos\dfrac{70°-40°}{2}}$

$= \dfrac{\sin 15°}{\cos 15°} = \tan 15° = \tan(45° - 30°)$

$= \dfrac{\tan 45° - \tan 30°}{1 + \tan 45° \tan 30°}$

Trigonometry (Functions & Identities) 9
Prove that, $\dfrac{1+\cos x+\sin x}{1-\cos x+\sin x} = \cot\dfrac{x}{2}$.

139

Hint

$$\frac{1+\cos x + \sin x}{1-\cos x + \sin x}$$
$$= \frac{2\cos^2\frac{x}{2} + 2\sin\frac{x}{2}\cos\frac{x}{2}}{2\sin^2\frac{x}{2} + 2\sin\frac{x}{2}\cos\frac{x}{2}}$$

Trigonometry (Functions & Identities) 10

If $\tan\theta = \frac{\sin\alpha - \cos\alpha}{\sin\alpha + \cos\alpha}$,

then show that, $\sin\alpha + \cos\alpha = \sqrt{2}\cos\theta$.

Hint

$$\tan\theta = \frac{\sin\alpha - \cos\alpha}{\sin\alpha + \cos\alpha} = \frac{\cos\alpha(\tan\alpha - 1)}{\cos\alpha(\tan\alpha + 1)}$$
$$= \frac{\tan\alpha - \tan\frac{\pi}{4}}{1 + \tan\alpha\tan\frac{\pi}{4}}$$

Trigonometry (Functions & Identities) 11

If $\cos(\theta + \phi) = m\cos(\theta - \phi)$,

then show that, $\tan\theta = \frac{1-m}{1+m}\cot\phi$.

Hint

$\cos(\theta + \phi) = m\cos(\theta - \phi)$

Or, $\frac{\cos(\theta + \phi)}{\cos(\theta - \phi)} = m$

Using componendo and dividendo

$$\frac{\cos(\theta - \phi) - \cos(\theta + \phi)}{\cos(\theta - \phi) + \cos(\theta + \phi)} = \frac{1-m}{1+m}$$

PROBLEMS IN SCHOOL MATHEMATICS

Trigonometry (Functions & Identities) 12
If $\tan A = \frac{1}{2}$ and $\tan B = -\frac{3}{14}$,
then show that, $\tan(2A + 3B) = -\frac{3}{14}$.

Hint

$$\tan(2A + 3B) = \frac{\tan 2A + \tan 3B}{1 - \tan 2A \tan 3B}$$

$$= \frac{\frac{2 \tan A}{1 - \tan^2 A} + \frac{3 \tan B - \tan^3 B}{1 - 3 \tan^2 B}}{1 - \frac{2 \tan A}{1 - \tan^2 A} \times \frac{3 \tan B - \tan^3 B}{1 - 3 \tan^2 B}}$$

Trigonometry (Functions & Identities) 13
Prove that, $\frac{\sin 16\theta \cos 2\theta - \sin 12\theta \cos 6\theta}{\cos 4\theta \cos 2\theta - \sin 6\theta \sin 8\theta} = \frac{4 \tan \theta (1 - \tan^2 \theta)}{1 - 6 \tan^2 \theta + \tan^4 \theta}$.

Hint

$$\frac{\sin 16\theta \cos 2\theta - \sin 12\theta \cos 6\theta}{\cos 4\theta \cos 2\theta - \sin 6\theta \sin 8\theta}$$

$$= \frac{\frac{1}{2}(\sin 18\theta + \sin 14\theta) - \frac{1}{2}(\sin 18\theta + \sin 6\theta)}{\frac{1}{2}(\cos 6\theta + \cos 2\theta) - \frac{1}{2}(\cos 2\theta - \cos 14\theta)}$$

$$= \frac{\sin 14\theta - \sin 6\theta}{\cos 6\theta + \cos 14\theta}$$

$$= \frac{2 \cos 10\theta \sin 4\theta}{2 \cos 10\theta \cos 4\theta}$$

$$= \tan 4\theta$$

$$= \tan 2(2\theta)$$

Trigonometry (Functions & Identities) 14
Prove that, $\frac{\sin \theta + \cos \theta}{\cos \theta - \sin \theta} + \frac{\cos \theta - \sin \theta}{\sin \theta + \cos \theta} = \frac{2}{\cos 2\theta}$.

Hint

$$\frac{\sin\theta + \cos\theta}{\cos\theta - \sin\theta} + \frac{\cos\theta - \sin\theta}{\sin\theta + \cos\theta}$$
$$= \frac{(\sin\theta + \cos\theta)^2 + (\cos\theta - \sin\theta)^2}{(\cos\theta)^2 - (\sin\theta)^2}$$

Trigonometry (Functions & Identities) 15

Prove that, $\sin(A+B)\sin(A-B) = \sin^2 A - \sin^2 B$
and $\cos(A+B)\cos(A-B) = \cos^2 A - \sin^2 B$.

Hint

$\sin(A+B)\sin(A-B)$
$= (\sin A \cos B + \cos A \sin B)(\sin A \cos B - \cos A \sin B)$
and $\cos(A+B)\cos(A-B)$
$= (\cos A \cos B - \sin A \sin B)(\cos A \cos B + \sin A \sin B)$

Trigonometry (Functions & Identities) 16

Prove that, $\dfrac{(\sin\theta + \cos\theta)^2 - 1}{(\cos\theta + \sin\theta)(\cos\theta - \sin\theta)} = \tan 2\theta$.

Hint

$$\frac{(\sin\theta + \cos\theta)^2 - 1}{(\cos\theta + \sin\theta)(\cos\theta - \sin\theta)}$$
$$= \frac{\sin^2\theta + 2\sin\theta\cos\theta + \cos^2\theta - 1}{\cos^2\theta - \sin^2\theta}$$

Trigonometry (Functions & Identities) 17

If $(A + B + C) = 180°$, then show that,
$\tan A + \tan B + \tan C = \tan A \tan B \tan C$.

PROBLEMS IN SCHOOL MATHEMATICS

Hint

$$\tan(A+B+C) = \frac{\tan(A+B)+\tan C}{1-\tan(A+B)\tan C}$$

Or, $\tan 180° = \dfrac{\frac{\tan A + \tan B}{1-\tan A \tan B} + \tan C}{1 - \frac{\tan A + \tan B}{1-\tan A \tan B} \times \tan C}$

Or, $0 = \dfrac{\tan A + \tan B + \tan C - \tan A \tan B \tan C}{1 - \tan B \tan C - \tan C \tan A - \tan A \tan B}$

Trigonometry (Inverse Functions) 18

Prove that, $\sin^{-1}\dfrac{4}{5} + \cos^{-1}\dfrac{12}{13} = \tan^{-1}\dfrac{63}{16}$.

Hint

Let $\sin^{-1}\dfrac{4}{5} = x$ and $\cos^{-1}\dfrac{12}{13} = y$

$\therefore \sin x = \dfrac{4}{5}, \cos x = \dfrac{3}{5}, \tan x = \dfrac{4}{3}$

and $\cos y = \dfrac{12}{13}, \sin y = \dfrac{5}{13}, \tan y = \dfrac{5}{12}$

Trigonometry (Inverse Functions) 19

Prove that, $\cot^{-1}\left(\dfrac{\sqrt{1+\sin x} + \sqrt{1-\sin x}}{\sqrt{1+\sin x} - \sqrt{1-\sin x}}\right) = \dfrac{x}{2}$, $x \in \left(0, \dfrac{\pi}{4}\right)$.

Hint

$$\sqrt{1+\sin x} = \sqrt{\sin^2 \frac{x}{2} + \cos^2 \frac{x}{2} + 2\sin\frac{x}{2}\cos\frac{x}{2}}$$

$$= \sin\frac{x}{2} + \cos\frac{x}{2}$$

$$\sqrt{1-\sin x} = \sqrt{\sin^2 \frac{x}{2} + \cos^2 \frac{x}{2} - 2\sin\frac{x}{2}\cos\frac{x}{2}}$$

$$= \sin\frac{x}{2} - \cos\frac{x}{2}$$

Trigonometry (Inverse Functions) 20

If $sin^{-1}(1-x) - 2\,sin^{-1} x = \frac{\pi}{2}$, then find the value of x?

Hint

$sin^{-1}(1-x) = \frac{\pi}{2} + 2\,sin^{-1} x$

Or, $sin\{sin^{-1}(1-x)\} = sin\left(\frac{\pi}{2} + 2\,sin^{-1} x\right)$

Or, $(1-x) = cos(2\,sin^{-1} x)$

Trigonometry (Applications) 21

An earthing wire connected to the top of an electric pole has its other end inside the ground. The foot of the wire is 3 m away from the pole and wire is making angle of 30° with the level of the ground. Determine the height of the pole?

Hint

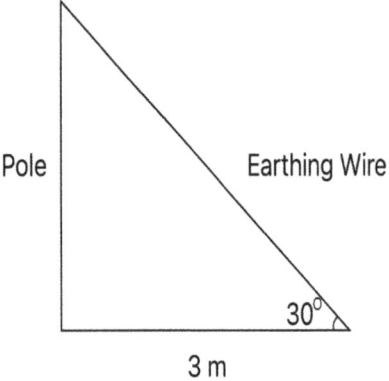

PROBLEMS IN SCHOOL MATHEMATICS

Trigonometry (Applications) 22
Javed is 1.5 m tall and is standing 12 m away from a tower. The angle of elevation from his eye to the top of the tower is 60°. Find the height of the tower?

Hint

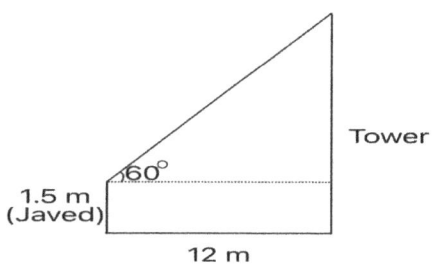

Trigonometry (Applications) 23
The angle of elevation of the top of an unfinished building of a point distant 90 m from its base is 15°. How much higher must the tower be raised so that the angle of elevation of the top of the finished building at same point will be 60°?

Hint

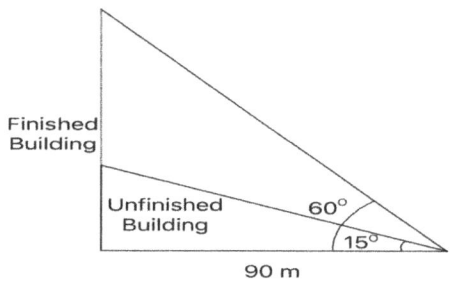

Trigonometry (Applications) 24

Two ladies Papiya and Purbasha on either side of a tower 100m high observed that the angles of elevation of the top of the tower to be 60° and 75°. What is the distance between them?

Hint

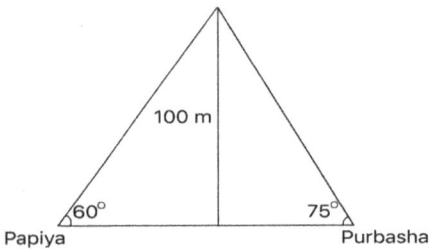

Trigonometry (Applications) 25

An aeroplane flying at a height of 500 m above the ground passes vertically above another plane at an instant when the angles of elevation of the two planes from the same point on the ground are 45° and 30° respectively. What is the height of the lower plane from the ground?

Hint

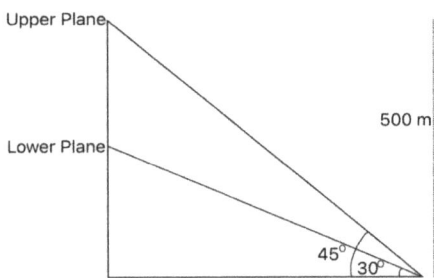

Trigonometry (Applications) 26

The heights of two towers are 70 m and 50 m. The line joining their tops make an angle 30° with the horizontal, then find the distance between the two towers?

Hint

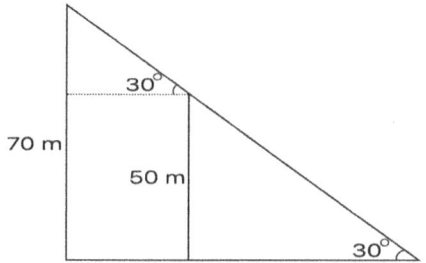

Trigonometry (Applications) 27

Bardhan was standing on the top of a rock cliff facing the sea. He saw a boat coming towards the rock. As he kept seeing time just flew. Five minutes less than half an hour, the angle of depression changed from 45° and 60°. How much more time will the boat take to reach the rock cliff?

Hint

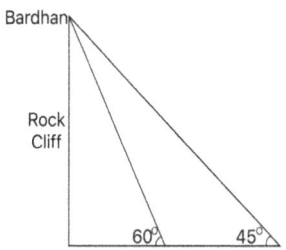

PROBLEMS IN SCHOOL MATHEMATICS

Trigonometry (Applications) 28
The angle of elevation of a cloud from a point 100 m above a lake is 45° and the angle of depression of its reflection in the lake is 60°. Find the height of the cloud?
Hint

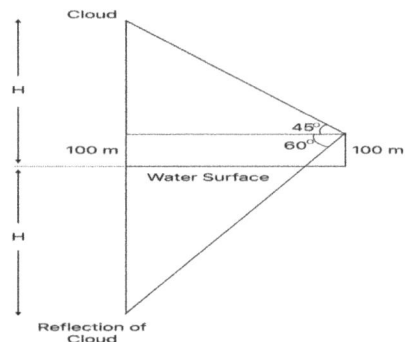

Trigonometry (Applications) 29
Prithwiraj standing in one corner of a square football field observes that the angle subtended by a pole in the corner just diagonally opposite to this corner is 45°. When he retires 60 m from the corner, along the same straight line, he finds the angle to be 30°. Find the length of the field?
Hint

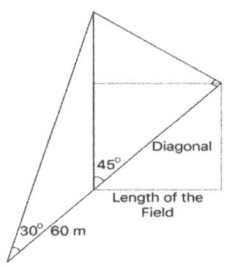

Trigonometry (Applications) 30

At the foot of a mountain, the elevation of its summit is 30°. After ascending 1 km towards the mountain upon an incline of 15°, the angle of elevation changes to 45°. Find the height of the mountain?

Hint

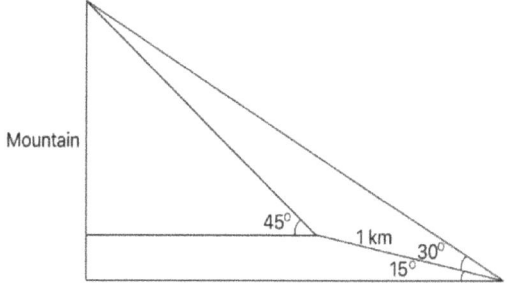

CALCULUS

8. Calculus
Calculus is a branch of mathematics that deals with the study of change and motion. Here are different branches of calculus:

Differential Calculus:
Focus: Concerned with the concept of the derivative, which represents the rate of change of a function with respect to a variable.
Key Concepts: Derivatives, slopes of curves, rate of change, tangents to curves.
Applications: Physics (e.g., velocity, acceleration), optimization problems, economics (e.g., marginal cost).

Integral Calculus:
Focus: Involves the concept of integral, with represents the accumulation of quantities, such as areas under curves on total accumulated values.
Key Concepts: Integrals, area under curves, anti-derivatives, definite and indefinite integrals.
Applications: Finding areas, volumes, and solving problems involving accumulation, like total distance travelled.

Multivariable Calculus:
Focus: Extends differential and integral calculus to functions of several variables.
Key Concepts: Partial derivatives, multiple integrals, gradient, divergence, curl and vector calculus.

Applications: *3D modelling, physics, engineering, economics.*

Vector Calculus:

Focus: *Deals with vector fields and operations on vectors in calculus.*

Key Concepts: *Gradient, divergence, curl, line integrals, surface integrals, Green's theorem, Stoke's theorem.*

Applications: *Fluid dynamics, electromagnetism, field theory.*

Differential Calculus:

Focus: *Involves equations that describe how functions are changed, typically involving derivatives.*

Key Concepts: *Ordinary differential equations (ODEs), partial differential equations (PDEs), solutions of differential equations.*

Applications: *Modelling dynamic systems in engineering, physics, biology, economics.*

Calculus of Variations:

Focus: *Deals with optimizing functions, typically integrals involving unknown functions.*

Key Concepts: *Euler-Lagrange equation, functional derivatives, minimization of functions.*

Applications: *Physics, economics, engineering.*

8.1. (Calculus) Limits

A limit is a fundamental concept used to describe the value that a function (or sequence) approaches as the input (or index) approaches a certain value.

Sum Rule:
$$\lim_{x \to c}(f(x) + g(x)) = \lim_{x \to c} f(x) + \lim_{x \to c} g(x)$$

Difference Rule:
$$\lim_{x \to c}(f(x) - g(x)) = \lim_{x \to c} f(x) - \lim_{x \to c} g(x)$$

Product Rule:
$$\lim_{x \to c}(f(x).g(x)) = \lim_{x \to c} f(x) . \lim_{x \to c} g(x)$$

Quotient Rule: *(Provided $\lim_{x \to c} g(x) \neq 0$)*
$$\lim_{x \to c} \frac{f(x)}{g(x)} = \frac{\lim_{x \to c} f(x)}{\lim_{x \to c} g(x)}$$

Constant Multiple Rule:
$$\lim_{x \to c} k.f(x) = k. \lim_{x \to c} f(x)$$

Limit of a Constant:
$$\lim_{x \to c} k = k$$

Limit of x:
$$\lim_{x \to c} x = c$$

Limit of x^n:
$$\lim_{x \to c} x^n = c^n$$

Limit of Exponential Functions:
$$\lim_{x \to c} e^x = e^c$$

Limit of Trigonometric Functions:
$$\lim_{x \to 0} \frac{\sin x}{x} = 1$$

Limit for any Positive Integer n:
$$\lim_{x \to a} \frac{x^n - a^n}{x - a} = na^{n-1}$$

L'Hôpital's Rule:
If $\lim_{x \to c} f(x) = 0$ and $\lim_{x \to c} g(x) = 0$ or both limits equal ∞, and if the derivatives $f'(x)$ and $g'(x)$ exist near c (expect possible at c), then:
$\lim_{x \to c} \frac{f(x)}{g(x)} = \lim_{x \to c} \frac{f'(x)}{g'(x)}$, provided that the limit on the right side exists or approaches $\pm \infty$.

8.2. (Calculus) Differential Calculus
The derivative of a function $f(x)$ at a point $x = a$ is defined as $f'(a) = \lim_{h \to 0} \frac{f(a+h) - f(a)}{h}$.

Rolle's Theorem:
If a function f satisfy the following conditions:
  I.   **Continuous on a Closed Interval:** f is continuous on the closed interval $[a, b]$.
  II. **Differentiable on the Open Interval:** f is differentiable on the open interval (a, b).
  III. **Equal Values at Endpoints:** $f(a) = f(b)$

Then, there exists at least one point c in the open interval (a, b) such that: $f'(c) = 0$

Lagrange Mean Value Theorem:
If a function f satisfy the following conditions:
  I.   **Continuous on a Closed Interval:** f is continuous on the closed interval $[a, b]$.
  II. **Differentiable on the Open Interval:** f is differentiable on the open interval (a, b).

Then, there exists at least one point c in the open interval (a, b) such that: $f'(c) = \frac{f(b) - f(a)}{b - a}$

Cauchy Mean Value Theorem:
If two functions f and g satisfy the following conditions:
- I. **_Continuous on a Closed Interval:_** Both f and g are continuous on the closed interval $[a, b]$.
- II. **_Differentiable on the Open Interval:_** Both f and g are differentiable on the open interval (a, b).

Then, there exists at least one point $c \in (a, b)$ such that:
$$\frac{f'(c)}{g'(c)} = \frac{f(b)-f(a)}{g(b)-g(a)}, \text{ where } g'(c) \neq 0$$

Power Rule:
For function $f(x) = x^n$, where n is any real number.
$f'(x) = nx^{n-1}$

Constant Rule:
For a constant function $f(x) = c$, where c is a constant.
$f'(x) = 0$

Sum/Difference Rule:
For functions $f(x) = g(x) \pm h(x)$
$f'(x) = g'(x) \pm h'(x)$

Product Rule:
- I. For functions $f(x) = g(x).h(x)$
$f'(x) = g'(x).h(x) + g(x).h'(x)$
- II. For functions $f(x) = u(x).v(x).w(x) \ldots$
$f'(x) = u'(x).v(x).w(x)\ldots + v'(x)u(x).w(x)\ldots + w'(x)u(x).v(x)\ldots$

Quotient Rule:
For function $f(x) = \frac{g(x)}{h(x)}$
$$f'(x) = \frac{g'(x).h(x) - g(x)h'(x)}{[h(x)]^2}$$

PROBLEMS IN SCHOOL MATHEMATICS

Chain Rule:
$f(x) = g(h(x))$
$f'(x) = g'(h(x)) \cdot h'(x)$

Derivative of Trigonometric Functions:
$f(x) = \sin(x), f'(x) = \cos(x)$
$f(x) = \cos(x), f'(x) = -\sin(x)$
$f(x) = \tan(x), f'(x) = \sec^2(x)$
$f(x) = \cot(x), f'(x) = -\operatorname{cosec}^2(x)$
$f(x) = \sec(x), f'(x) = \sec(x)\tan(x)$
$f(x) = \operatorname{cosec}(x), f'(x) = -\operatorname{cosec}(x)\cot(x)$

Derivative of Inverse Trigonometric Functions:
$f(x) = \sin^{-1}(x), f'(x) = \dfrac{1}{\sqrt{1-x^2}}, |x| < 1$

$f(x) = \cos^{-1}(x), f'(x) = -\dfrac{1}{\sqrt{1-x^2}}, |x| < 1$

$f(x) = \tan^{-1}(x), f'(x) = \dfrac{1}{1+x^2}$

$f(x) = \operatorname{cosec}^{-1}(x), f'(x) = -\dfrac{1}{|x|\sqrt{x^2-1}}, |x| > 1$

$f(x) = \sec^{-1}(x), f'(x) = \dfrac{1}{|x|\sqrt{x^2-1}}, |x| > 1$

$f(x) = \cot^{-1}(x), f'(x) = -\dfrac{1}{1+x^2}$

Derivative of Exponential Functions:
$f(x) = e^x, f'(x) = e^x$
$f(x) = a^x, f'(x) = a^x \ln(a)$ *(Where a is constant)*

Derivative of Logarithmic Functions:

$f(x) = ln(x), f'(x) = \dfrac{1}{x}$

$f(x) = log_a(x), f'(x) = \dfrac{1}{x \, ln(a)}$

Taylor Series:

$f(x) = f(a) + f'(a)(x - a) + \dfrac{f''(a)}{2!}(x - a)^2 + \ldots \ldots \ldots$

Maclaurin Series (Taylor Series around $a = 0$):

$f(x) = f(0) + f'(0)x + \dfrac{f''(0)}{2!}x^2 + \ldots \ldots \ldots$

8.3. (Calculus) Integral Calculus

Power Rule for Integration:

For $f(x) = x^n$, where $n \neq -1$:

$\displaystyle\int x^n dx = \dfrac{x^{n+1}}{n+1} + C$,

Where, C is a constant integration.

Integral of a Constant c:

$\displaystyle\int c \, dx = cx + C$,

Sum/Difference Rule:

For functions $f(x) = g(x) \pm h(x)$

$\displaystyle\int [g(x) \pm h(x)] dx = \int g(x) dx \pm \int h(x) dx$

Integration by Substitution (Change of Variable):

If $u = g(x)$, then:

$\displaystyle\int f(g(x)) g'(x) dx = \int f(u) du$

PROBLEMS IN SCHOOL MATHEMATICS

Integration by Parts:
For functions $u(x)$ and $v(x)$:
$$\int u(x)v'(x)dx = u(x)v(x) - \int v(x)u'(x)dx$$

Integral of Trigonometric Functions:

$$\int \sin(x)dx = -\cos(x) + C$$

$$\int \cos(x)dx = \sin(x) + C$$

$$\int \sec^2(x)dx = \tan(x) + C$$

$$\int \cosec^2(x)dx = -\cot(x) + C$$

$$\int \sec(x)\tan(x)dx = \sec(x) + C$$

$$\int \cosec(x)\cot(x)dx = -\cosec(x) + C$$

$$\int \tan(x)\,dx = \log|\sec x| + C$$

$$\int \cot(x)\,dx = \log|\sin x| + C$$

$$\int \sec(x)\,dx = \log|\sec x + \tan x| + C$$
$$= \log\left|\tan\left(\frac{\pi}{4}+\frac{x}{2}\right)\right| + C$$

$$\int \cosec(x)dx = \log|\cosec x - \cot x| + C$$
$$= \log\left|\tan\frac{x}{2}\right| + C$$

Integral Forms Involving Inverse Trigonometric Functions:

$$\int \frac{1}{\sqrt{1-x^2}} dx = \sin^{-1}(x) + C \text{ or } -\cos^{-1}(x) + C, |x| < 1$$

$$\int \frac{1}{1+x^2} dx = \tan^{-1}(x) + C \text{ or } -\cot^{-1}(x) + C$$

$$\int \frac{1}{x\sqrt{x^2-1}} dx = \sec^{-1}(x) + C \text{ or } -\csc^{-1}(x) + C, |x| > 1$$

Integral of Inverse Trigonometric Functions:

$$\int \sin^{-1}(x) dx = x \sin^{-1}(x) + \sqrt{1-x^2} + C, |x| \leq 1$$

$$\int \cos^{-1}(x) dx = x \cos^{-1}(x) - \sqrt{1-x^2} + C, |x| \leq 1$$

$$\int \tan^{-1}(x) dx = x \tan^{-1}(x) - \frac{1}{2} \ln(1+x^2) + C$$

$$\int \cot^{-1}(x) dx = x \cot^{-1}(x) + \frac{1}{2} \ln(1+x^2) + C$$

$$\int \sec^{-1}(x) dx = x \sec^{-1}(x) - \ln\left|x + \sqrt{x^2-1}\right| + C, |x| \geq 1$$

$$\int \csc^{-1}(x) dx = x \csc^{-1}(x) + \ln\left|x + \sqrt{x^2-1}\right| + C, |x| \geq 1$$

Integral of Exponential Functions:

$$\int e^x dx = e^x + C$$

$\int a^x dx = \frac{a^x}{\ln(a)} + C$, (a is a constant.)

Integral of Logarithmic Functions:

$\int \frac{1}{x} dx = \ln|x| + C$

PROBLEMS IN SCHOOL MATHEMATICS

Some Special Integrals

$$\int \frac{dx}{x^2 + a^2} = \frac{1}{a} \tan^{-1}\left(\frac{x}{a}\right) + C$$

$$\int \frac{dx}{x^2 - a^2} = \frac{1}{2a} \log \left|\frac{x - a}{x + a}\right| + C$$

$$\int \frac{dx}{a^2 - x^2} = \frac{1}{2a} \log \left|\frac{a + x}{a - x}\right| + C$$

$$\int \frac{dx}{\sqrt{a^2 - x^2}} = \sin^{-1}\left(\frac{x}{a}\right) + C$$

$$\int \frac{dx}{\sqrt{x^2 + a^2}} = \log \left|x + \sqrt{x^2 + a^2}\right| + C$$

$$\int \frac{dx}{\sqrt{x^2 - a^2}} = \log \left|x + \sqrt{x^2 - a^2}\right| + C$$

$$\int \sqrt{a^2 - x^2}\, dx = \frac{x}{2}\sqrt{a^2 - x^2} + \frac{a^2}{2} \sin^{-1}\left(\frac{x}{a}\right) + C$$

$$\int \sqrt{x^2 + a^2}\, dx = \frac{x}{2}\sqrt{x^2 + a^2} + \frac{a^2}{2} \log \left|x + \sqrt{x^2 + a^2}\right| + C$$

$$\int \sqrt{x^2 - a^2}\, dx = \frac{x}{2}\sqrt{x^2 - a^2} - \frac{a^2}{2} \log \left|x + \sqrt{x^2 - a^2}\right| + C$$

Integration of Rational Functions:
(Partial Function Decomposition)

For rational functions, need to decompose the function into simpler fractions and then integrate term by term.

Step-by-Step Guide to Partial Function Decomposition:

➢ Identify the Rational Function

$R(x) = \frac{P(x)}{Q(x)}$, Where $P(x)$ and $Q(x)$ are polynomials.

➢ Ensure Proper Form

If the degree of $P(x)$ is greater than or equal to degree of $Q(x)$:

$R(x) = D(x) + \frac{R_1(x)}{Q(x)}$, Where $D(x)$ is the quotient and $R_1(x)$ is a polynomial with a lower degree than $Q(x)$.

> Factor the Denominator

$Q(x) = (x - r_1)(x - r_2)(x^2 + bx + c) \ldots \ldots \ldots$

> Set Up the Partial Fraction Decomposition

$$\frac{P(x)}{Q(x)} = \frac{A_1}{(x - r_1)} + \frac{A_2}{(x - r_2)} + \ldots + \frac{Ax + B}{(x^2 + bx + c)} + \ldots \ldots$$

> Clear the Denominator

Multiply both sides by $Q(x)$:

$$P(x) = A_1(x - r_2)(x^2 + bx + c) \\ + A_2(x - r_1)(x^2 + bx + c) + \ldots \ldots \ldots$$

> Expand and Collect Like Terms
> Solve for Coefficients

Definite Integral:

The definite integral of $f(x)$ from a to b is given by:

$\int_a^b f(x)dx = F(b) - F(a)$, $F(x)$ is the anti-derivatives of $f(x)$.

8.4. (Calculus) Differential Equations
General Form of a Differential Equation:
Ordinary Differential Equation (ODE):

$F(x, y, y', y'', \ldots \ldots \ldots y^{(n)}) = 0$,

Where $y' = \frac{dy}{dx}$, $y'' = \frac{d^2y}{dx^2}$, etc.

Partial Differential Equation (PDE):

$F\left(x_1, x_2, \ldots \ldots, x_n, u, \frac{du}{dx_1}, \frac{du}{dx_2}, \ldots \ldots \frac{du}{dx_n}, \ldots\right)$

Where, $u = u(x_1, x_2, \ldots\ldots\ldots, x_n)$.

First-order Differential Equations:

Separable Differential Equation:

$$\frac{dy}{dx} = g(x)h(y)$$

Solution:

$$\int \frac{1}{h(y)} dy = \int g(x) dx + C$$

Linear First-order Differential Equation:

$$\frac{dy}{dx} + P(x)y = Q(x)$$

Solution:

$$y(x) = e^{-\int p(x)dx} \left[\int Q(x) e^{\int p(x)dx} dx + C \right]$$

Exact Differential Equation:

$$M(x, y)dx + N(x, y)dy = 0$$

Where equation is exact if $\frac{dM}{dy} = \frac{dN}{dx}$.

Solution:

Find a function $\Psi(x, y)$ such that:

$$\frac{d\Psi}{dx} = M(x, y), \frac{d\Psi}{dy} = N(x, y)$$

Second Order Differential Equations:

Homogeneous Linear Second-order Differential Equation:

$$\frac{d^2y}{dx^2} + p(x)\frac{dy}{dx} + q(x)y = 0$$

Solution:

If y_1 and y_2 are independent solutions, the general is
$y(x) = C_1 y_1(x) + C_2 y_2(x)$

Non-homogeneous Linear Second-order Differential Equation:
$$\frac{d^2y}{dx^2} + p(x)\frac{dy}{dx} + q(x)y = f(x)$$
Solution:
The general solution is the sum of the complementary (homogeneous) solution y_c and a particular solution y_p:
$$y(x) = y_c(x) + y_p(x)$$

Special Differential Equations:
Bernoulli's Equation:
$$\frac{dy}{dx} + P(x)y = Q(x)y^n$$
Solution:
Introduce $v = y^{1-n}$, transforming it into a linear differential equation.

Euler-Cauchy Equation:
$$x^2\frac{d^2y}{dx^2} + ax\frac{dy}{dx} + by = 0$$
Solution:
Use the substitution $x = e^t$, leading to a linear equation with constant coefficient.

Higher-order Differential Equations:
$$\frac{d^ny}{dx^n} + a_{n-1}(x)\frac{d^{n-1}y}{dx^{n-1}} + \ldots\ldots\ldots + a_1(x)\frac{dy}{dx} + a_0(x)y = g(x)$$

Solution:
Similar to second-order complementary (homogeneous) and particular solutions

8.5. (Calculus) Formulas from Calculus and their Applications

Rate of Change Formula: *The derivative of a function gives the rate of change of the function with respect to the independent value.*

If $y = f(x)$, then the derivative $f'(x) = \frac{dy}{dx}$, gives the rate at which y changes with x.

Slope of a Tangent Line: *The derivative of a function at a point gives the slope of the tangent line to the curve at that point.*

$$f'(a) = \lim_{h \to 0} \frac{f(a+h) - f(a)}{h}$$

Higher-order Derivatives: *The second, third, etc; derivatives of a function represent the rate of change of the first, second, etc; derivatives.*

If $y = f(x)$, then the second derivative is $f''(x) = \frac{d^2y}{dx^2}$, the third derivative is $f'''(x) = \frac{d^3y}{dx^3}$, and so on.

Maxima and Minima (Optimization Problems): *The derivative can be used to find critical points, which help in identifying local maxima and minima.*

Critical points occur where $f'(x) = 0$ or $f'(x)$ does not exist. The second derivative test can confirm whether these points are maxima or minima.

Linear Approximation (Differentials): *The derivative is used to approximate small changes in a function.*

$\Delta y \approx f'(x_0) \Delta x$, where Δx is a small change in x.

PROBLEMS IN SCHOOL MATHEMATICS

Area under a Curve (Single Function): *When calculating the area under a curve represented by a function $f(x)$ over an interval $[a, b]$, the area is given by:*
$A = \int_a^b f(x)\, dx$

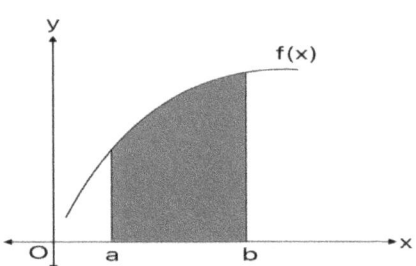

Area between two Curves: *If you want to find the area*

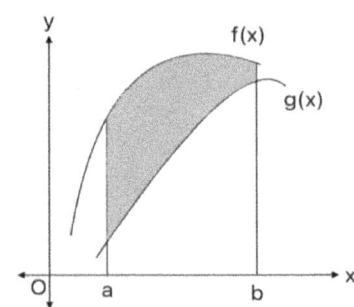

between two curves $f(x)$ and $g(x)$ on the interval $[a, b]$, where $f(x) \geq g(x)$ for all x in that interval, the area is given by:
$A = \int_a^b (f(x) - g(x))\, dx$

Area of a Region Bounded by Parametric Equation: *When a curve is defined parametrically by $x = f(t)$ and $y = g(t)$ over some parameter interval $[t_1, t_2]$, the area under the curve can be calculated by the formula:*
$A = \int_{t_1}^{t_2} y(t) \dfrac{dx}{dt}\, dt$

PROBLEMS IN SCHOOL MATHEMATICS

Area in Polar Coordinates: For curves described in polar coordinates by $r = f(\theta)$, the area of the region bounded by the curve and the radial lines at angles θ_1 and θ_2 is given by:
$$A = \frac{1}{2}\int_{\theta_1}^{\theta_2} r^2 d\theta$$

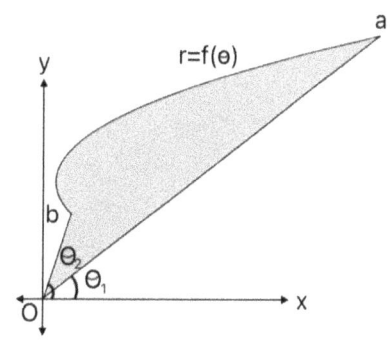

Area of a Surface Revolution: If you revolve a curve $f(x)$ around the x-axis, the surface area of the generated shape can be computed using:

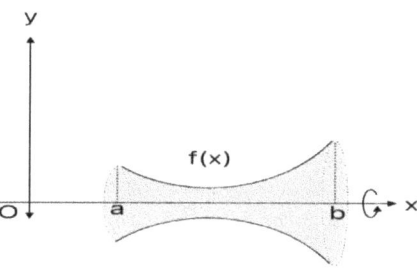

$$A = 2\pi \int_a^b f(x)\sqrt{1 + (f'(x))^2}\, dx$$

PROBLEMS IN SCHOOL MATHEMATICS

Problems

Calculus (Limits) 1

Evaluate, $\lim\limits_{x \to 0} \dfrac{xe^x + \log_e(1-x)}{x^2}$.

Hint

$\lim\limits_{x \to 0} \dfrac{xe^x + \log_e(1-x)}{x^2} \left(form \dfrac{0}{0}\right)$

$= \lim\limits_{x \to 0} \dfrac{xe^x + e^x - \dfrac{1}{1-x}}{2x} \left(form \dfrac{0}{0}\right)$

$= \lim\limits_{x \to 0} \dfrac{xe^x + e^x + e^x - \dfrac{1}{(1-x)^2}}{2}$

Calculus (Limits) 2

Evaluate, $\lim\limits_{x \to 0} \dfrac{(1-\cos 2x) \sin^2 \dfrac{x}{2}}{x^3}$.

Hint

$\lim\limits_{x \to 0} \dfrac{(1-\cos 2x) \sin^2 \dfrac{x}{2}}{x^3} \left(form \dfrac{0}{0}\right)$

$= \lim\limits_{x \to 0} \dfrac{2\sin^2 x \cdot \dfrac{(1-\cos x)}{2}}{x^3}$

$\left(\begin{array}{c} formula\ used, \\ 1 - \cos 2x = 2\sin^2 x\ and\ 1 - \cos x = 2\sin^2 \dfrac{x}{2} \end{array}\right)$

$= \lim\limits_{x \to 0} \dfrac{\sin x}{x} \cdot \lim\limits_{x \to 0} \dfrac{\sin x}{x} \cdot \lim\limits_{x \to 0} \dfrac{1 - \cos x}{x}$

PROBLEMS IN SCHOOL MATHEMATICS

Calculus (Derivatives) 3
Find $\frac{dy}{dx}$, $x^a \cdot y^b = (x+y)^{a+b}$.

Hint

$$\frac{d}{dx}(x^a \cdot y^b) = \frac{d}{dx}(x+y)^{a+b}$$

Or, $x^a \cdot \frac{d}{dy}y^b \cdot \frac{dy}{dx} + y^b \cdot \frac{d}{dx}x^a = (a+b)(x+y)^{a+b-1} \cdot \frac{d}{dx}(x+y)$

Calculus (Derivatives) 4
Differentiate $\log\left\{e^x \left(\frac{x-2}{x+2}\right)^{\frac{3}{4}}\right\}$ with respect to x.

Hint

$$\log\left\{e^x \left(\frac{x-2}{x+2}\right)^{\frac{3}{4}}\right\}$$

$$= \log e^x + \frac{3}{4}\log\left(\frac{x-2}{x+2}\right)$$

Calculus (Derivatives) 5
Find $\frac{dy}{dx}$, $y = \frac{1}{\sqrt{n^2-m^2}}\log\frac{\sqrt{n+m}+\sqrt{n-m}\tan\frac{x}{2}}{\sqrt{n+m}-\sqrt{n-m}\tan\frac{x}{2}}$.

Hint

$$\frac{1}{\sqrt{n^2-m^2}}\log\frac{\sqrt{n+m}+\sqrt{n-m}\tan\frac{x}{2}}{\sqrt{n+m}-\sqrt{n-m}\tan\frac{x}{2}}$$

$$= \frac{1}{\sqrt{n^2-m^2}}\left[\log\left(\sqrt{n+m}+\sqrt{n-m}\tan\frac{x}{2}\right) - \log\left(\sqrt{n+m}-\sqrt{n-m}\tan\frac{x}{2}\right)\right]$$

PROBLEMS IN SCHOOL MATHEMATICS

Calculus (Derivatives) 6
Find $\frac{dy}{dx}$, $x^y + y^x + x^x + y^y = a^b$.
Hint
Let $t = x^y, u = y^x, v = x^x, w = y^y$, then take logarithm on both sides.

Calculus (Derivatives) 7
Find $\frac{dy}{dx}$, $y = x + \cfrac{1}{x + \cfrac{1}{x + \cfrac{1}{x + \dots}}}$.
Hint
$$y = x + \frac{1}{y}$$

Calculus (Derivatives) 8
Find $\frac{dy}{dx}$, $y = (\sin x \cos x)^{(\sin x \cos x)^{(\sin x \cos x)^{\dots\infty}}}$.
Hint
$y = (\sin x \cos x)^y$

Calculus (Derivatives) 9
Find $\frac{dy}{dx}$, $y = \sqrt{\tan x + \sqrt{\tan x + \sqrt{\tan x \dots}}}$.
Hint
$y = \sqrt{\tan x + y}$

Calculus (Derivatives) 10
Find $\frac{dy}{dx}$, $y = \sin^{-1}\left(\frac{e^{abx} - e^{-abx}}{e^{abx} + e^{-abx}}\right)$.

PROBLEMS IN SCHOOL MATHEMATICS

Hint

Let $\dfrac{e^{abx} - e^{-abx}}{e^{abx} + e^{-abx}} = m$

Calculus (Derivatives) 11

Find $\dfrac{dy}{dx}$, $y = \tan^{-1}\left\{\dfrac{\sqrt{1+x} - \sqrt{1-x}}{\sqrt{1+x} + \sqrt{1-x}}\right\}$.

Hint

Let $x = \cos 2\theta$

Calculus (Derivatives) 12

Find $\dfrac{dy}{dx}$, $\tan^{-1}\left(\dfrac{3y^2 x - x^3}{y^3 - 3yx^2}\right)$, $-\dfrac{1}{\sqrt{3}} < \dfrac{x}{y} < \dfrac{1}{\sqrt{3}}$.

Hint

Let $\dfrac{x}{y} = \tan\theta$

Calculus (Integrals) 13

Integrate, $\displaystyle\int \dfrac{\sqrt{x^2+1}\,[\log(x^2+1) - 2\log x]}{x^4}\,dx$.

Hint

$\displaystyle\int \dfrac{\sqrt{x^2+1}\,[\log(x^2+1) - 2\log x]}{x^4}\,dx$

$= \displaystyle\int \dfrac{1}{x^3}\sqrt{\dfrac{x^2+1}{x^2}}\left[\log\left(1 + \dfrac{1}{x^2}\right)\right]dx$

Let $\dfrac{x^2+1}{x^2} = t$

Calculus (Integrals) 14

Integrate, $\displaystyle\int e^{-9x} \sin^3 x\,dx$.

PROBLEMS IN SCHOOL MATHEMATICS

Hint

$$\int e^{-9x} \sin^3 x \, dx$$

$$= \sin^3 x \int e^{-9x} dx - \int \left(\frac{d}{dx} \sin^3 x \int e^{-9x} dx\right) dx$$

Calculus (Integrals) 15

Integrate, $\int \frac{(\cot \theta + \cot^3 \theta)}{(1 + \cot^3 \theta)} d\theta$.

Hint

$$\frac{(\cot \theta + \cot^3 \theta)}{(1 + \cot^3 \theta)}$$

$$= \frac{\cot \theta (1 + \cot^2 \theta)}{(1 + \cot^3 \theta)}$$

Let $\cot \theta = t$, where $1 + \cot^2 \theta = \text{cosec}^2 \theta$

Calculus (Integrals) 16

Integrate, $\int e^{3x} \sin^2 x \cos^3 x \, dx$.

Hint

$e^{3x} \sin^2 x \cos^3 x$

$$= \frac{e^{3x}}{4} (2 \sin x \cos x)^2 \cos x$$

$$= \frac{e^{3x}}{4} \sin^2 2x \cos x$$

$$= \frac{e^{3x}}{8} (1 - \cos 4x) \cos x$$

$$= \frac{1}{16} (2e^{3x} \cos x - e^{3x} \cos 3x - e^{3x} \cos 5x)$$

PROBLEMS IN SCHOOL MATHEMATICS

Calculus (Integrals) 17
Integrate, $\int \frac{x^2}{(x-1)^4(x^3+1)} dx$.

Hint

Let $x - 1 = t$

Calculus (Integrals) 18
Integrate, $\int \frac{x^4 + 4x^3 + 11x^2 + 12x + 8}{(x^2 + 2x + 3)^2(x+1)} dx$.

Hint

$$\frac{x^4 + 4x^3 + 11x^2 + 12x + 8}{(x^2 + 2x + 3)^2(x + 1)} = \frac{Ax + B}{(x^2 + 2x + 3)^2} + \frac{Cx + D}{(x^2 + 2x + 3)} + \frac{E}{(x + 1)}$$

Calculus (Integrals) 19
Integrate, $\int 7^{7^{7^{7^x}}} 7^{7^{7^x}} 7^{7^x} 7^x \, dx$.

Hint

Let $7^{7^{7^{7^x}}} = t$

Calculus (Integrals) 20
Integrate, $\int \frac{1}{x \log x \log(\log x) \log[\log(\log x)]} dx$.

Hint

Let $\log x = t$

Calculus (Integrals) 21
Integrate, $\int_{\log \sqrt{3}}^{\log \sqrt{5}} \frac{1}{(e^{ax} + e^{-ax})(e^{ax} - e^{-ax})} dx$.

PROBLEMS IN SCHOOL MATHEMATICS

Hint

$$\frac{1}{(e^{ax} + e^{-ax})(e^{ax} - e^{-ax})}$$
$$= \frac{1}{(e^{2ax} - e^{-2ax})}$$
$$= \frac{e^{2ax}}{(e^{2ax})^2 - 1}$$
Let $e^{2ax} = t$

Calculus (Integrals) 22
Integrate, $\int_0^{\frac{\pi}{2}} \frac{dx}{(m^2 \cos^2 x + n^2 \sin^2 x)^2}$.

Hint

Divide numerator and denominator by $\cos^4 x$ and put $\tan x = t$.

Calculus (Differential Equations) 23
Solve, $\frac{y^{99}}{x^{99}} \frac{dy}{dx} + \frac{x^{100} + y^{100} - 1}{2(x^{100} + y^{100}) + 1} = 0$.

Hint

Let $x^{100} + y^{100} = t$

Or, $100x^{99} + 100y^{99} \frac{dy}{dx} = \frac{dt}{dx}$

Or, $1 + \frac{y^{99}}{x^{99}} \frac{dy}{dx} = \frac{1}{100x^{99}} \frac{dt}{dx}$

Calculus (Differential Equations) 24
Solve, $(y + xy^2) dx + (x - x^2 y) dy = 0$.

Hint
Integrating factor $= \dfrac{1}{(y+xy^2)x - (x-x^2y)y}$

Calculus (Differential Equations) 25
Solve, $\dfrac{dy}{dx} - x\sin 2y = x^3 \sin^2 y$.

Hint
$\dfrac{dy}{dx} - x\sin 2y = x^3 \sin^2 y$

Or, $\cosec^2 y \dfrac{dy}{dx} - \dfrac{2\sin y \cos y}{\sin^2 y} x = x^3$

Or, $\cosec^2 y \dfrac{dy}{dx} + (-\cot y)2x = x^3$

Let $-\cot y = t$

So, $\cosec^2 y \dfrac{dy}{dx} = \dfrac{dt}{dx}$

$\therefore \dfrac{dt}{dx} + 2xt = x^3$

Integration factor $= e^{\int 2x\, dx}$

Calculus (Differential Equations) 26
Solve,
$(50x^2 + 50y^2 + x)\,dx - (100x^2 + 100y^2 - y)\,dy = 0$.

Hint
$(50x^2 + 50y^2 + x)\,dx - (100x^2 + 100y^2 - y)\,dy = 0$

Or, $[50(x^2+y^2) + x]\,dx - [100(x^2+y^2) - y]\,dy = 0$

Or, $\left[50 + \left\{\dfrac{x}{(x^2+y^2)}\right\}\right]dx + \left[\left\{\dfrac{y}{(x^2+y^2)}\right\} - 100\right]dy = 0$

$\therefore \dfrac{d}{dy}\left[50 + \left\{\dfrac{x}{(x^2+y^2)}\right\}\right] = \dfrac{d}{dx}\left[\left\{\dfrac{y}{(x^2+y^2)}\right\} - 100\right] = \dfrac{-2xy}{(x^2+y^2)^2}$

173

Calculus (Differential Equations) 27

Solve, $\frac{d^n y}{dx^n} = \left(\frac{d^{n-1} y}{dx^{n-1}}\right)^n$.

Hint

$$\frac{d^n y}{dx^n} = \left(\frac{d^{n-1} y}{dx^{n-1}}\right)^n$$

Or, $\frac{d}{dx}\left(\frac{d^{n-1} y}{dx^{n-1}}\right) = \left(\frac{d^{n-1} y}{dx^{n-1}}\right)\left(\frac{d^{n-1} y}{dx^{n-1}}\right)^{n-1}$

Or, $\frac{d\left(\frac{d^{n-1} y}{dx^{n-1}}\right)}{\frac{d^{n-1} y}{dx^{n-1}}} = \left(\frac{d^{n-1} y}{dx^{n-1}}\right)^{n-1} dx$

Calculus (Applications) 28

Find the greatest volume of cylinder which can inscribed in a sphere of radius R.

Hint

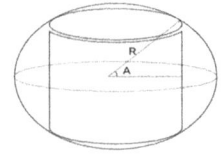

Radius of cylinder $= R \cos A$
Height of cylinder $= 2R \sin A$
Volume$(V) = \pi \times (R \cos A)^2 \times 2R \sin A$
Or, $V = 2\pi R^3 (1 - \sin^2 A) \sin A$

$\therefore \frac{dV}{dA} = 2\pi R^3 \left[\frac{d}{dA} \sin A - \frac{d}{dA} \sin^3 A\right]$

Calculus (Applications) 29

Find the area bounded by the parabolas

PROBLEMS IN SCHOOL MATHEMATICS

$x^2 = 4ay, y^2 = 4ax$ (where $a > 0$) and the circle $x^2 + y^2 = a^2$?

Hint

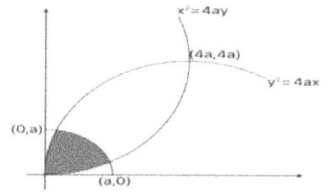

Calculus (Applications) 30

The population of a certain country is known to increase at a rate of proportional to the number of people presently living in the country. If after ten years the population is doubled, and after 15 years the population is 1,00,000, estimate the number of people initially living in the country.

Hint

Let the number of people living in the country at time 't' = N

Number of people initially living in the country = N_0

$\dfrac{dN}{dt} = kN$ (where k is proportionality constant)

The solution is, $N = ce^{kt}$

At, $t = 0, N = N_0$

So, $c = N_0$

$\therefore N = N_0 e^{kt}$

At $t = 10, N = 2N_0$

$\therefore 2N_0 = N_0 e^{10k}$

Or, $k = \dfrac{1}{10} \log_e 2$

PROBLEMS IN SCHOOL MATHEMATICS

VECTOR ALGEBRA

9. Vector Algebra

A vector is a mathematical entity characterized by both magnitude (length) and direction. It can be represented in various forms, such as coordinates in a coordinate system. Vectors are often denoted by boldface letters or with an arrow on top.

9.1. (Vector Algebra) Types of Vectors

Zero Vector *(Null Vector): A vector with zero magnitude and no direction.*

Unit Vector: *A vector with a magnitude 1.*

Position Vector: *A vector representing the position of a point relative to the origin.*

Collinear Vectors: *Vectors that lie along the same line or parallel lines.*

Equal Vectors: *Vectors with the same magnitude and direction, even if their initial point are different.*

Co-initial Vectors: *Vectors that start from the same initial point but may have different directions or magnitudes.*

Displacement Vector: *A vector representing the shortest distance between two points, indicating both magnitude and direction.*

Concurrent Vectors: *Vectors that passes through the same point, through may have different directions.*

Orthogonal Vectors (Perpendicular Vectors): *Vectors that are at right angles to each other.*

Free Vector: *A vector that can be moved parallel to itself without changing its properties.*

Negative Vector: *A vector that has the same magnitude but the opposite direction to a given vector.*

Coplanar Vectors: *Vectors that lie in the same plane.*

9.2. (Vector Algebra) Operations on Vectors

Addition:

$\vec{u} + \vec{v} = (u_1 + v_1, u_2 + v_2, \ldots\ldots\ldots)$

Subtraction:

$\vec{u} - \vec{v} = (u_1 - v_1, u_2 - v_2, \ldots\ldots\ldots)$

Scalar Multiplication:

$k\vec{v} = (kv_1, kv_2, \ldots\ldots\ldots)$

Dot Product (Scalar Product):

$\vec{u} \cdot \vec{v} = |\vec{u}||\vec{v}| \cos\theta$

Properties:

Commutative: $\vec{u} \cdot \vec{v} = \vec{v} \cdot \vec{u}$

Distributive: $\vec{u} \cdot (\vec{v} + \vec{w}) = \vec{u} \cdot \vec{v} + \vec{u} \cdot \vec{w}$

Linear in each Argument: $(a\vec{u}) \cdot \vec{v} = a(\vec{u} \cdot \vec{v})$, *where a is a scalar.*

Cross Product (Vector Product):

$|\vec{u} \times \vec{v}| = |\vec{u}||\vec{v}| \sin\theta$

Properties:

Not Commutative: $\vec{u} \times \vec{v} = -(\vec{v} \times \vec{u})$

Distributive: $\vec{u} \times (\vec{v} + \vec{w}) = (\vec{u} \times \vec{v} + \vec{u} \times \vec{w})$

Scalar Multiple:

$(k\vec{u}) \times \vec{v} = k(\vec{u} \times \vec{v})$

Magnitude (Norm) of a Vector:
$$|\vec{v}| = \sqrt{v_1^2 + v_2^2 + \ldots\ldots\ldots + v_n^2}$$

Unit Vector:
$$\hat{v} = \frac{\vec{v}}{|\vec{v}|}$$

Vector Projection:
Projection of $\vec{u}$ onto $\vec{v} = \dfrac{\vec{u}.\vec{v}}{|\vec{v}|^2}\vec{v}$

Vector Triple Product:
$$\vec{u} \times (\vec{v} \times \vec{w}) = (\vec{u}.\vec{w})\vec{v} - (\vec{u}.\vec{v})\vec{w}$$

Angle between Two Vectors:
$$\theta = \cos^{-1}\left(\frac{\vec{u}.\vec{v}}{|\vec{u}||\vec{v}|}\right)$$

9.3. (Vector Algebra) Vector Calculus Identities

Gradient:
The gradient of a scalar function f is a vector field:
$$\nabla f = \left(\frac{\partial f}{\partial x}, \frac{\partial f}{\partial y}, \frac{\partial f}{\partial z}\right)$$

Divergence:
The divergence of a vector field $A = (A_x, A_y, A_z)$ is a scalar field:
$$\nabla.A = \frac{\partial A_x}{\partial x} + \frac{\partial A_y}{\partial y} + \frac{\partial A_z}{\partial z}$$

Curl:
The curl of a vector field $A = (A_x, A_y, A_z)$ is a vector field:
$$\nabla \times A = \left(\frac{\partial A_z}{\partial y} - \frac{\partial A_y}{\partial z}, \frac{\partial A_x}{\partial z} - \frac{\partial A_z}{\partial x}, \frac{\partial A_y}{\partial x} - \frac{\partial A_x}{\partial y}\right)$$

Laplacian:

The Laplacian of a scalar field f is:
$$\nabla^2 A = \nabla \cdot \nabla f = \frac{\partial^2 f}{\partial x^2} + \frac{\partial^2 f}{\partial y^2} + \frac{\partial^2 f}{\partial z^2}$$
The Laplacian of a vector field f is:
$$\nabla^2 A = (\nabla^2 A_x, \nabla^2 A_y, \nabla^2 A_z)$$

Product Rule Identities:

Gradient of a product (scalar functions f and g):
$$\nabla(fg) = f\nabla g + g\nabla f$$
Divergence of a product (scalar f and vector A):
$$\nabla \cdot (fA) = f(\nabla \cdot A) + A \cdot \nabla f$$
Curl of a product (scalar f and vector A):
$$\nabla \times (fA) = f(\nabla \times A) - A \times \nabla f$$

Divergence of the Curl:

The divergence of the curl of any vector field A is always zero:
$$\nabla \cdot (\nabla \times A) = 0$$

Curl of the Gradient:

The curl of the gradient of any scalar function f is always zero:
$$\nabla \times (\nabla f) = 0$$

Laplacian of a Product:

For scalar functions f and g:
$$\nabla^2(fg) = f\nabla^2 g + 2(\nabla f \cdot \nabla g) + g\nabla^2 f$$

PROBLEMS IN SCHOOL MATHEMATICS

Problems

Vector Algebra 1
If A, B and C are the vertices of a triangle ABC, then prove that $\dfrac{a}{\sin A} = \dfrac{b}{\sin B} = \dfrac{c}{\sin C}$.

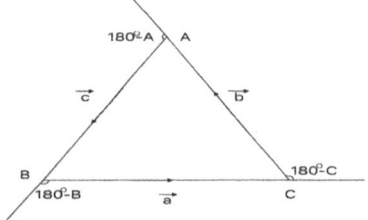

Hint
$$\vec{a} + \vec{b} = -\vec{c}$$
$$Or, \vec{a} \times \vec{a} + \vec{a} \times \vec{b} = -\vec{a} \times \vec{c}$$
$$Or, 0 + \vec{a} \times \vec{b} = \vec{c} \times \vec{a}$$

Or, $|\vec{a} \times \vec{b}| = |\vec{c} \times \vec{a}|$
Or, $ab \sin(180° - C) = ca \sin(180° - B)$
Or, $ab \sin C = ca \sin B$
Or, $\dfrac{b}{\sin B} = \dfrac{c}{\sin C}$

Vector Algebra 2
A vector $\vec{r}$ inclined at equal angles to the three axes. If the magnitude of $\vec{r}$ is $\sqrt{3}$ units, then find the value of $\vec{r}$.

Hint
Equal inclined, so direction cosines are same.
$$l = m = n = \pm \frac{1}{\sqrt{3}}$$
$$\therefore \vec{r} = \hat{r}|\vec{r}| = \left| \pm \frac{1}{\sqrt{3}}\hat{i} \pm \frac{1}{\sqrt{3}}\hat{j} \pm \frac{1}{\sqrt{3}}\hat{k} \right| \sqrt{3}$$

PROBLEMS IN SCHOOL MATHEMATICS

Vector Algebra 3
Using vectors prove that parallelogram on the same base and between the same parallels are equal in area.

Hint
$area(parallelogram\ ABCD) = \vec{a} \times \vec{b}$
$area(parallelogram\ CDFE) = \overrightarrow{CD} \times \overrightarrow{CE}$
$= \overrightarrow{CD} \times (\overrightarrow{CB} + \overrightarrow{BE}) =$
$\vec{a} \times (\vec{b} + k\vec{a})$
$= (\vec{a} \times \vec{b}) + k(\vec{a} \times \vec{a})$

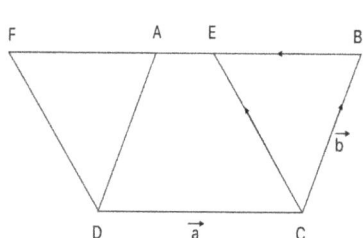

Vector Algebra 4
Prove that in any $\triangle ABC$, $\cos A = \dfrac{b^2 + c^2 - a^2}{2bc}$, where a, b and c are the magnitudes of the sides opposite to the vertices A, B and C respectively.

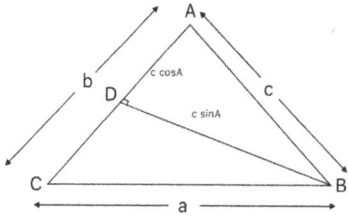

Hint
$CD = b - c \cos A$
Applying Pythagoras,
$(CB)^2 = (CD)^2 + (BD)^2$

Vector Algebra 5

If $\vec{a}, \vec{b}$ and $\vec{c}$ are three mutually perpendicular vectors of the same magnitude, prove that $(\vec{a} + \vec{b} + \vec{c})$ is equally inclined to the vectors $\vec{a}, \vec{b}$ and $\vec{c}$. Also find these angles.

Hint

Let $|\vec{a}| = |\vec{b}| = |\vec{c}| = x$

$\vec{a}.\vec{b} = \vec{b}.\vec{c} = \vec{c}.\vec{a} = 0$ *(Mutually perpendicular vectors)*

$\therefore |\vec{a} + \vec{b} + \vec{c}|^2 = \vec{a}.\vec{a} + \vec{b}.\vec{b} + \vec{c}.\vec{c} + 2(\vec{a}.\vec{b} + \vec{b}.\vec{c} + \vec{c}.\vec{a})$

$$= |\vec{a}|^2 + |\vec{b}|^2 + |\vec{c}|^2$$
$$= 3x^2$$

So, $|\vec{a} + \vec{b} + \vec{c}| = \sqrt{3}x$

Let $(\vec{a} + \vec{b} + \vec{c})$ makes angles α, β and γ with $\vec{a}, \vec{b}$ and $\vec{c}$ respectively.

$(\vec{a} + \vec{b} + \vec{c}).\vec{a} = |\vec{a} + \vec{b} + \vec{c}||\vec{a}|\cos \alpha$
$$= \sqrt{3}x^2 \cos \alpha$$

$\therefore |\vec{a}|^2 = \sqrt{3}x^2 \cos \alpha$

Or, $x^2 = \sqrt{3}x^2 \cos \alpha$

Or, $\cos \alpha = \frac{1}{\sqrt{3}}$

$\therefore \alpha = \beta = \gamma = \cos^{-1}\left(\frac{1}{\sqrt{3}}\right)$

Vector Algebra 6

Prove that $|\vec{a} \times \vec{b}|^2 = \begin{vmatrix} \vec{a}.\vec{a} & \vec{a}.\vec{b} \\ \vec{a}.\vec{b} & \vec{b}.\vec{b} \end{vmatrix}$.

PROBLEMS IN SCHOOL MATHEMATICS

Hint

$$|\vec{a} \times \vec{b}|^2 = (\vec{a} \times \vec{b}).(\vec{a} \times \vec{b})$$
$$= (ab\sin\theta)\hat{n}.(ab\sin\theta)\hat{n}$$
$$= (a^2b^2\sin^2\theta)(\hat{n}.\hat{n})$$
$$= a^2b^2(1 - \cos^2\theta)$$
$$= a^2b^2 - a^2b^2\cos^2\theta$$
$$= (\vec{a}.\vec{a})(\vec{b}.\vec{b}) - (\vec{a}.\vec{b})^2$$

Vector Algebra 7

Using vectors prove that the line segment joining the midpoints of two sides of a triangle is parallel to the third side and equal to half of it.

Hint

$$\vec{DE} = \left(\frac{\vec{x} + \vec{z}}{2}\right) - \left(\frac{\vec{x} + \vec{y}}{2}\right)$$
$$= \frac{1}{2}(\vec{z} - \vec{y}) = \frac{1}{2}\vec{BC}$$

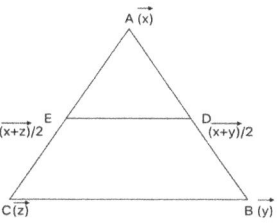

Vector Algebra 8

Using vectors prove that the diagonals of a quadrilateral bisect each other if it is a parallelogram.

Hint

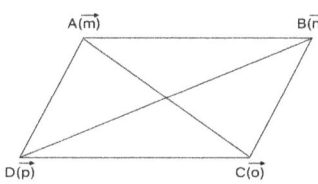

$$\vec{AB} = \vec{DC}$$
$$Or, (\vec{n} - \vec{m}) = (\vec{o} - \vec{p})$$
$$Or, \vec{n} + \vec{p} = \vec{o} + \vec{m}$$
$$Or, \frac{1}{2}(\vec{n} + \vec{p}) = \frac{1}{2}(\vec{o} + \vec{m})$$

Vector Algebra 9

Using vectors prove that if a, b and c are the lengths of three sides of a triangle, then its area is given by $\sqrt{s(s-a)(s-b)(s-c)}$, where $s = \frac{a+b+c}{2}$.

Hint

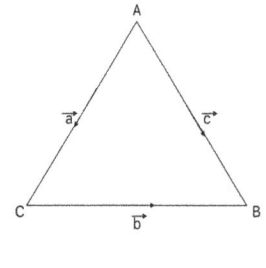

$$Area = \frac{1}{2}|\overrightarrow{CB} \times \overrightarrow{CA}|$$

$$= \frac{1}{2}|\vec{b} \times -\vec{a}|$$

$$= \frac{1}{2}|\vec{b} \times \vec{a}|$$

$\therefore 2Area = |\vec{b} \times \vec{a}|$

Or, $4(Area)^2 = |\vec{b} \times \vec{a}|^2$

Or, $4(Area)^2 = \{-(\vec{b}.\vec{a}) + |\vec{b}|^2|\vec{a}|^2\}$ *[Lagrange's identity]*

Or, $16(Area)^2 = 4|\vec{b}|^2|\vec{a}|^2 - \{-2(\vec{b}.\vec{a})\}^2$

Or, $16(Area)^2 = 4|\vec{b}|^2|\vec{a}|^2 - \{|\vec{b}|^2 + |\vec{a}|^2 - |\vec{b}+\vec{a}|^2\}^2$

Or, $16(Area)^2 = (2ba)^2 - \{|\vec{b}|^2 + |\vec{a}|^2 - |\vec{c}|^2\}^2$

[Where $\vec{a}+\vec{b}+\vec{c}=0$]

Or, $16(Area)^2 = (2ba)^2 - (b^2+a^2-c^2)^2$

Or, $16(Area)^2 = (2ba + b^2 + a^2 - c^2)(2ba - b^2 - a^2 + c^2)$

Or, $16(Area)^2 = [(a+b)^2 - c^2][c^2 - (a-b)^2]$

Or, $16(Area)^2 = (a+b+c)(a+b-c)(c+a-b)(c-a+b)$

Or, $16(Area)^2 = 2s(2s-2c)(2s-2b)(2s-2a)$

Vector Algebra 10

Using vectors prove that angle in a semicircle is a right angle.

Hint

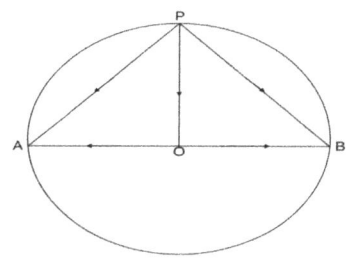

$$\overrightarrow{PA} = \overrightarrow{PO} + \overrightarrow{OA}$$
$$\overrightarrow{PB} = \overrightarrow{PO} + \overrightarrow{OB}$$
$$= \overrightarrow{PO} - \overrightarrow{OA} [Because\ \overrightarrow{OB} = -\overrightarrow{OA}]$$
$$\therefore \overrightarrow{PA}.\overrightarrow{PB} = (\overrightarrow{PO} + \overrightarrow{OA})(\overrightarrow{PO} - \overrightarrow{OA})$$
$$= |\overrightarrow{PO}|^2 - |\overrightarrow{OA}|^2$$
$$= 0\ [Because\ |\overrightarrow{PO}| = |\overrightarrow{OA}| = Radius]$$
$$\therefore \overrightarrow{PA} \perp \overrightarrow{PB}$$

PROBABILITY

10. Probability
Probability is a branch of mathematics that deals with likelihood of events occurring. It provides a measure of how likely an event is to happen, ranging from 0 (impossible) to 1 (certain).

10.1. (Probability) Basic Concepts
Experiment:
An action or process that leads to one or more outcomes
Outcome:
A possible result of an experiment
Event:
A set of all possible outcomes of an experiment

10.2. (Probability) Probability of an Event
The probability $P(A)$ of an event A is defined as:
$$P(A) = \frac{Number\ of\ Favourable\ Outcomes}{Total\ Number\ of\ Outcomes}$$

10.3. (Probability) Complementary Events
The probability of the complement of an event A (i.e., A^C), which is the event that A does not occur, is:
$P(A^C) = 1 - P(A)$

10.4. (Probability) Union of Events

For two events A and B, the probability of A or B occurring (union) is:

$P(A \cup B) = P(A) + P(B) - P(A \cap B)$

10.5. (Probability) Intersection of Events

The probability of both A and B occurring (intersection) is:

$P(A \cap B) = P(A) \times P(B)$, for independent events

10.6. (Probability) Conditional Probability

The probability of event A given that B has occurred is:

$P(A|B) = \dfrac{P(A \cap B)}{P(B)}$

10.7. (Probability) Baye's Theorem

Used to find the probability of an event based on prior knowledge of conditions related to the event:

$P(A|B) = \dfrac{P(B|A)P(A)}{P(B)}$

10.8. (Probability) Probability Distributions

Discrete Probability Distribution:

For discrete random variables, where outcomes are countable (e.g. rolling a die). The probability mass function gives the probability of each outcome.

Continuous Probability Distribution:

For continuous probability distributions describe the probabilities of outcomes for continuous random *variables, one that can take any value within a given range (e.g. heights of people). The probability density function provides probabilities over intervals.*

Binomial Distribution:

A binomial distribution is a type of probability distribution that models the number of successes in a fixed number of independent trials, where each trail has only two possible outcomes: success or failure.

$P(X = k) = \binom{n}{k} P^k (1-P)^{n-k}$, *n is the number of trails, k is the number of successes, and P is the probability of success.*

Normal Distribution:

A continuous distribution described by its mean μ and standard deviation σ. The probability density function is:

$$f(x) = \frac{1}{\sigma\sqrt{2\pi}} e^{-\frac{(x-\mu)^2}{2\sigma^2}}$$

10.9. (Probability) Expected Value and Variance

Expected Value (Mean):

$E(X) = \sum x_i \cdot P(x_i)$, *for discrete variables.*

$E(X) = \int x \cdot f(x) dx$, *for continuous variables.*

Variance:

$Var(X) = E\left[(X - E(X))^2\right]$

These fundamental concepts and formulas provide the basis for understanding and applying probability in various contexts, from simple games of chance to statistical analyses.

PROBLEMS IN SCHOOL MATHEMATICS

10.10. (Probability) Representations of Probability

Representation	Description	Visual Characteristics
Probability Density Function (PDF) / Probability Mass Function (PMF)	Shows probability distribution for continuous (PDF) or discrete (PMF) variables	A curve (PDF) or set of bars (PMF) over the x-axis values
Cumulative Distribution Functions (CDF)	Cumulative Probability up to a certain value	A curve rising from 0 to 1, never decreasing
Tree Diagram	Depicts possible outcomes of a sequence of events	A branching diagram with probabilities on each branch
Venn Diagram	Illustrates relationships between events, particularly overlap	Circles overlapping in different sections.
Bar Graph	Represents probabilities for discrete outcomes	Bars of different heights proportional to probability
Pie Chart	Shows proportion of probabilities within a whole	A circles divided into slices, proportional to the probabilities
Histogram	Shows frequency or probability distribution for continuous data	Bars where the area represents probability, continuous on the x-axis
Heat Map	Visualizes joint probability distribution for two variables	Grid of sequence where colour intensity represents probability
Scatter Plot with Shading	Displays data points with probability density shading	Scatter plot with colour gradients showing probability regions

PROBLEMS IN SCHOOL MATHEMATICS

Problems

Probability 1
A bag contains 10 green balls, 20 blue balls and 30 red balls. If five balls are picked at random, what is the probability that three of them are blue and two of them are red?
Hint
Probability = $(^{20}C_3 \times {}^{30}C_2)/{}^{60}C_5$

Probability 2
Find the probability of getting five heads when ten coins are tossed?
Hint
Probability = ${}^{10}C_5/2^{10}$

Probability 3
Two cards are drawn from pack of 52 cards. Find the probability that both are hearts or both are queens or both are red cards?
Hint
Probability = $({}^{13}C_2 + {}^{4}C_2 + {}^{26}C_2)/{}^{52}C_2$

Probability 4
What is the probability of choosing three distinct numbers randomly from (1, 2, 3 ....100) such that all are divisible by both 3 and 4?

PROBLEMS IN SCHOOL MATHEMATICS

Hint
Number divisible by both 3 and 4 from 1 to 100 = (12, 24, 36, 48, 60, 72, 84, 96)
Therefore, Probability = $^8C_3/^{100}C_3$

Probability 5
.A total of 20 members of Rabindra Sangha's play cricket, 15 play football, and 10 play rugby. Furthermore, 12 of the members play both cricket and football, 7 play both football and rugby, 5 play both rugby and cricket, and 3 play all three sports. How many members of this club play at least one of the three sports?

Hint
Numbers of members play at least one of the three sports = (Number of cricket players) + (Number of football players) + (Number of rugby players) - (Number of both cricket and football players) - (Number of both football and rugby players) - (Number of both rugby and cricket players) + (Number of players of all three sports)

Probability 6
Vivekananda Vidyapith consists of 60 teachers. If the school policy is to have 30 of the teachers taking classes, 10 of the teachers walking full time at the school's administration, and 20 of the teachers on reserve for next period. How many different divisions of 60 teachers into the 3 groups are possible?

PROBLEMS IN SCHOOL MATHEMATICS

Hint

$$\text{Possible division} = \frac{60!}{30!\, 10!\, 20!}$$

Probability 7

Priya is known to speak the truth 7 out of 10 times. She draws a card from a pack of 52 playing cards and reports that it is a diamond. Find the probability that it is actually a diamond?

Hint

Let E_1 be the event that the Priya reports that is a diamond and E be the event that a diamond occurs.

$P(E) = \dfrac{13}{52}$

$P(\bar{E}) = 1 - P(E)$

$P\left(\dfrac{E_1}{E}\right) = P(\text{Priya speaking the truth}) = \dfrac{7}{10}$

And $P\left(\dfrac{E_1}{\bar{E}}\right) = P(\text{Priya not speaking the truth}) = 1 - \dfrac{7}{10}$

Clearly, $\left(\dfrac{E}{E_1}\right)$ is the event that is actually a diamond, when it is known that Priya reports a diamond.

$$P\left(\dfrac{E}{E_1}\right) = \dfrac{P(E)\cdot P\left(\dfrac{E_1}{E}\right)}{P(E)\cdot P\left(\dfrac{E_1}{E}\right) + P(\bar{E})\cdot P\left(\dfrac{E_1}{\bar{E}}\right)}$$

PROBLEMS IN SCHOOL MATHEMATICS

Probability 8
What is the possibility of getting a sum of 27 or more when five dice are thrown?

Hint
Total number of ways $= 6^5$

Number of ways getting a sum 27
$(6, 6, 6, 6, 3) = \frac{5!}{4!\,1!}$

Or, $(6, 6, 6, 5, 4) = \frac{5!}{3!\,1!\,1!}$

Number of ways getting a sum 28
$(6, 6, 6, 6, 4) = \frac{5!}{4!\,1!}$

Or, $(6, 6, 6, 5, 5) = \frac{5!}{3!\,2!}$

Number of ways getting a sum 29 $(6, 6, 6, 6, 5) = \frac{5!}{4!\,1!}$

Number of ways getting a sum 30 $(6, 6, 6, 6, 6) = \frac{5!}{5!}$

Therefore, probability of getting sum 27 or more

$$= \frac{\frac{5!}{4!\,1!} + \frac{5!}{3!\,1!\,1!} + \frac{5!}{4!\,1!} + \frac{5!}{3!\,2!} + \frac{5!}{4!\,1!} + \frac{5!}{5!}}{6^5}$$

Probability 9
What is the probability of guessing correctly at least 95 out of 100 multiple choice questions of four options on an examination?

PROBLEMS IN SCHOOL MATHEMATICS

Hint

Probability
$= {}^{100}C_{95}\left(\frac{1}{4}\right)^{95}\left(\frac{1}{4}\right)^{5} + {}^{100}C_{96}\left(\frac{1}{4}\right)^{96}\left(\frac{1}{4}\right)^{4} + {}^{100}C_{97}\left(\frac{1}{4}\right)^{97}\left(\frac{1}{4}\right)^{3} + {}^{100}C_{98}\left(\frac{1}{4}\right)^{98}\left(\frac{1}{4}\right)^{2} + {}^{100}C_{99}\left(\frac{1}{4}\right)^{99}\left(\frac{1}{4}\right) + {}^{100}C_{100}\left(\frac{1}{4}\right)^{100}$

$= \left(\frac{1}{4}\right)^{100} ({}^{100}C_{95} + {}^{100}C_{96} + {}^{100}C_{97} + {}^{100}C_{98} + {}^{100}C_{99} + {}^{100}C_{10}$

Probability 10

From Manu's past experience in Jampui, she known it rains 1 in 10 days. When it rains, she observes 80% of the people carry umbrellas. When it is not raining only 20% of the people carry umbrellas. Manu notice Ishu walking in with an umbrella. What's the probability that it's raining?

PROBLEMS IN SCHOOL MATHEMATICS

Hint
Let R be the event of raining and R_1 be the event of carry an umbrella.

$P(R) = \dfrac{1}{10}$

$P(\bar{R}) = 1 - P(R)$

$P\left(\dfrac{R_1}{R}\right) = P(Carry\ the\ umbrella\ when\ raining) = 80\% = \dfrac{4}{5}$

$P\left(\dfrac{R_1}{\bar{R}}\right) = P(Carry\ the\ umbrella\ when\ not\ raining) = 20\%$

$\qquad = \dfrac{1}{5}$

Clearly, $P\left(\dfrac{R}{R_1}\right)$ is the event that is actually raining, when Ishu carry the umbrella.

$P\left(\dfrac{R}{R_1}\right) = \dfrac{P(R).P\left(\dfrac{R_1}{R}\right)}{P(R).P\left(\dfrac{R_1}{R}\right) + P(\bar{R}).P\left(\dfrac{R_1}{\bar{R}}\right)}$

MATHEMATICAL NOTATIONS

$+$	Plus
$-$	Minus
$\cdot$ or $\times$	Multiplication
$/$ or $\div$	Division
$\pm$	PlusMinus
$\mp$	MinusPlus
$\%$	Percent
$\sqrt{}$	Square Root
$=$	Equal
$\neq$	Not Equal
$\approx$	Approximately Equal
$\sim$	Similarity or Proportionality
$\propto$	Proportional To
$\equiv$	Identical To
$\cong$	Congruent To
$<$	Less Than
$>$	Greater Than
$\leq$	Less Than or Equal To
$\geq$	Greater Than or Equal To
$\ll$	Much Less Than
$\gg$	Much Greater Than
$\emptyset$	Empty Set
$\#$	Number Sign
$\in$	Belongs To
$\notin$	Not Belongs To
$\ni$	Contains As Members
$\subset$	Subset Of
$\cup$	Union
$\cap$	Intersection
$\forall$	For All
Δ	Increment
$\exists$	There Exists
$\sum$	Sum Of
$\prod$	Product Of
$\Rightarrow$	Implication
$\Leftrightarrow$	Logical Equivalence
$!$	Factorial
$\circ$	Function Composition
$\oplus$	Exclusive Or
$\ominus$ or $\triangle$	Symmetric Difference
$\perp$	Perpendicular
$\parallel$	Parallel
∞	Infinity

Graph Type	Description
Linear Graph	A straight line graph that represents a linear equation, where the slope of the line indicates the rate of change.
Quadratic Graph	A parabola shaped graph representing a quadratic equation. The curve can open upwards and downwards based on the coefficient of x^2.
Cubic Graph	A curve that can change direction up to two times, representing a cubic equation. The curve is more complex and can cross the x-axis up to three times.
Exponential Graph	A curve that shows rapid increase or decrease, representing an exponential function. The graph rises (or falls) sharply.
Logarithmic Graph	A curve that increases quickly and then slows down, representing a logarithmic function. The inverse of exponential growth.
Sine Wave	A periodic graph that represents the sine function, oscillating between maximum and minimum values at regular interval.
Cosine Wave	Similar to sine wave, but starts at maximum value. Represents the cosine function.
Tangent Graph	Periodic graph asymptotes, representing the tangent function. The graph repeats every π unit.
Absolute Value Graph	A V-shaped graph representing the absolute value function, reflecting all negative values to positive.
Logistic Graph	An S-shaped curve representing logistic growth.

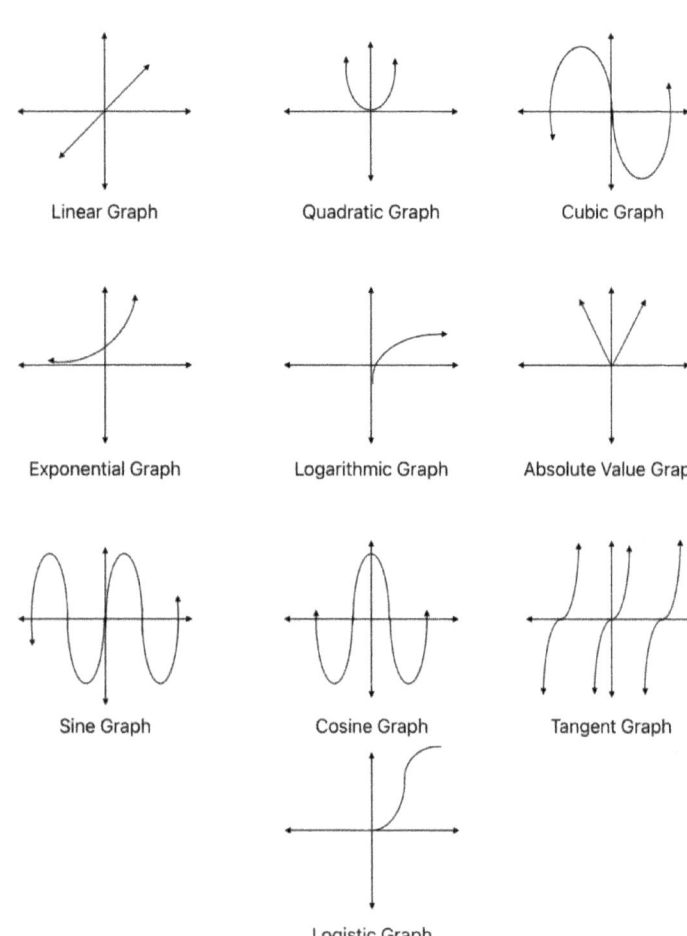

Paradox	Description	Key Concept
Zeno's Paradoxes	A set of paradoxes arguing that motion and change are illogical	Infinite Division, Limits
Russell's Paradox	A set that contains all sets that do not contain themselves creates a logical contradiction	Self-reference, Inconsistency in Set Theory
Monty Hall Problem	Switching doors after one is revealed increases your chances of winning from 1/3 to 2/3	Conditional Probability, Decision Theory
Banach-Tarski Paradox	A solid sphere can be divided and reassembled into two identical spheres	Non-Euclidean Geometry, Axiom of Choice
The Barber Paradox	A barber shaves everyone who doesn't shave themselves; does the barber shave himself	Self-reference, Contradiction
The Liar Paradox	A statement that says, "This statement is false," creating a contradiction if it's either true or false	Self-reference, Truth Paradox
Galileo's Paradox	There are as many squares as there are natural numbers, even though most numbers are not perfect squares	Infinity, One-to-One Correspondence
Simpson's Paradox	A trend appears in different groups of data but reverses or disappears when the groups are combined	Conditional Probability, Aggregation Bias
The Twin Paradox	In special relativity, one twin ages slower than the other when travelling at near-light speed	Time Dilation, Relativity of Simultaneity
Hilbert's Hotel	An infinity hotel can still accommodate more guests, even when fully occupied	Infinity, Infinite Sets

"Mathematics is the queen of sciences, and arithmetic is the queen of mathematics." **-Carl Friedrich Gauss**

"Mathematics is the language with which God has written the universe."
-Blaise Pascal

"Mathematics possesses not only truth, but also supreme beauty."
-Leonhard Euler

"The laws of nature are but the mathematical thoughts of God." **-Euclid**

"Pure mathematics is, in the way, the poetry of logical ideas." **-Albert Einstein**

"An equation for me has no meaning unless it expresses a thought of God."
-Srinivasa Ramanujan

"Mathematics knows no races or geographic boundaries; for mathematics, the cultural world is one country."**-David Hilbert**

"There is geometry in the humming of the strings; there is music in the spacing of the spheres." **-Pythagoras**

"A mathematician is a device for turning coffee into theorems." **-Paul Erdős**

"Mathematics is the most beautiful and most powerful creation of the human spirit." **-Stefan Banach**

"It is impossible to be a mathematician without being a poet in soul."
-Sofia Kovalevskaya

"Nature is written in mathematical language." **-Galileo Galilei**

"The essence of mathematics lies in the freedom." **-Georg Cantor**

"The study of mathematics, like the Nile, begins in minuteness but ends in magnificence." **-Charles Caleb Colton**

"Without mathematics, there's nothing you can do. Everything around you is mathematics. Everything around you is numbers." **-Shakuntala Devi**

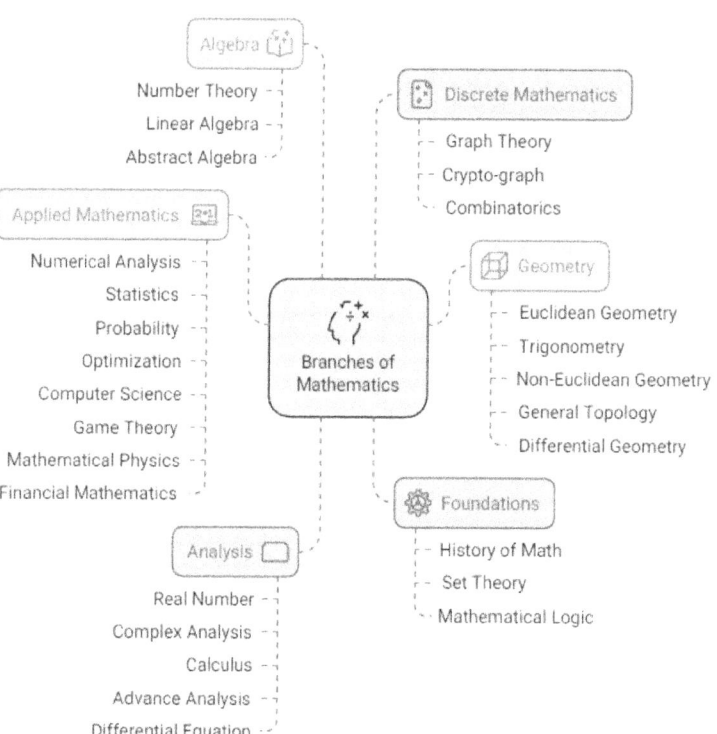

www.ingramcontent.com/pod-product-compliance
Lightning Source LLC
LaVergne TN
LVHW061611070526
838199LV00078B/7241